NEW FIRST CERTIFICATE ENGLISH
Book 1

Language
and
Composition

W S Fowler and J Pidcock

Thomas Nelson and Sons Ltd
Nelson House Mayfield Road
Walton-on-Thames Surrey KT12 5PL

51 York Place
Edinburgh EH1 3JD

P.O. Box 18123
Nairobi Kenya

Yi Xiu Factory Building
Unit 05-06 5th Floor
65 Sims Avenue Singapore 1438

Thomas Nelson (Hong Kong) Ltd
Toppan Building 10/F
22A Westlands Road
Quarry Bay Hong Kong

Thomas Nelson (Nigeria) Ltd
8 Ilupeju Bypass
PMB 21303 Ikeja Lagos

First published by
Thomas Nelson and Sons Ltd 1984

ISBN 0-17-555444-7

NCN 719-9041-0

Printed in Great Britain by
Butler & Tanner Ltd, Frome and London

NEW FIRST CERTIFICATE ENGLISH
Book 1

Language and Composition

W S Fowler and J Pidcock

Nelson

Contents

Stage Two

Passive forms and usage; prepositions of time; defining and non-defining relative clauses; **where** (relative adverb); Past Simple, **used to** and **would**

had better and **should (ought to)**; **unless** and **provided**; prepositions of place; **have/get something done**

Conditional sentences (1); **must** (logical conclusion and obligation); purpose clauses (1)

Uses of tenses - Present and Future; future time clauses; **in case**; question tags

Statements; imperative forms for command and request; questions

Use and omission of the definite article; relative clauses using prepositions

Stage Three

Introduction

● *New First Certificate English*

Since its publication in 1973–5, *First Certificate English* has been the course most widely used by students preparing for the Cambridge examination at this level. In these ten years, however, English teaching methodology has changed considerably, and now the examination itself is to be modified, with effect from June 1984. In preferring to write a new course, which will be published to coincide with the appearance of the new examination, rather than to revise the original, my co-authors, John Pidcock and Robert Rycroft, and I have been primarily concerned to take these changes in methodology into account. Over 90% of the material in the course is new.

While this was in our view a necessary step, it does not mean that the examination as such has changed to a noticeable extent either in level or form, except in the design of the aural/oral tests (covered by Book 4 of the new course). The main reasons for changes in approach, primarily intended to shift the emphasis away from the remedial teaching of grammar towards the acquisition of skills, are the following: first, students entering a First Certificate course nowadays have in most cases been taught differently from those who entered them ten years ago; secondly, we ourselves, after ten years' further experience of teaching Cambridge examination classes, have modified our own ideas.

● The design of the course

The four books comprising the new course can be used independently in order to concentrate on a specific paper in the examination, but they have been written in such a way that they relate to each other. The 24 units of *Book 1, Language and Composition* are reinforced by 24 parallel units in *Book 2, Reading Comprehension*, each of which develops through passages and exercises the themes and lexis contained in the corresponding unit in *Book 1*. The grammatical structures emphasised in given units of *Book 1* are further practised and employed in structural exercises in *Book 3, Use of English*, and the subjects for guided composition, which form Section B of the Use of English paper, are similarly related to group work tasks in *Book 1* in most cases. There is a clear cross-reference index at the end of this book, referring to *Book 3*, which shows how exercises there can be used for remedial work and reinforcement of what has been taught. Although dialogue is no longer one of the composition forms required by the examination, the relationship between written and spoken English is still of maximum importance inside and outside the classroom. Consequently, many of the texts in this book are in dialogue form, and their themes are expanded in listening material provided in *Book 4, Listening Comprehension and Interview*.

● The organisation of the units in *Book 1*

Book 1 of the course contains 24 units, each of six pages, and is divided into four stages, each stage having six units. The units reflect the different kinds of composition students may be asked to write, and there is therefore a progression in four stages of increasing difficulty for each type, both in terms of the development of writing skills and of the grammatical content.

Four of the six types are specifically indicated in the Cambridge syllabus: description (which comes first at each stage and is therefore found in Units 1, 7, 13 and 19); discussion (which comes third); narrative (fifth); and prescribed books (sixth). The last-named unit at each stage is included for the benefit of those students who intend to answer the optional question on a prescribed book in the examination. While these units may be of interest to students in general, they will have no direct application for them unless they are studying a set book. Since it is impossible to predict which book students may choose in a given year, and which books will be replaced at the end of the year by the examiners, the units are designed to teach the most effective techniques for dealing with novels or plays set, irrespective of the choice that has been made.

While students are no longer required to write dialogue, composition topics may be set that do not fall precisely into the categories already mentioned. Apart from that, it must be remembered that Cambridge First Certificate is not an end in itself for the majority of students but should be seen as part of a continuing process of learning English. It is a serious mistake, for this reason, to imagine that the best way to reach the First Certificate standard is simply to study old examination papers; what is necessary, instead, is to learn the skills required to reach this standard, and in so doing, develop one's command of English for a wider application of it. The even-numbered units in this book, apart from those devoted to prescribed books, are therefore intended to deal with the English required for communication in the widest possible sense of the word, ranging from asking the way to expressing wishes and regrets, from inviting someone to a party to apologising for mistakes, from planning holidays or business trips to writing letters of complaint.

● **The relationship between skills and grammatical accuracy**

The principal emphasis in this book is on acquiring the skills necessary to write English in a wide variety of circumstances, any one of which may be tested in the examination. This is in part a matter of learning appropriate techniques and suitable forms of expression, but it also depends on the ability to link together successfully the relevant structures that have been learnt in previous years. Since students may have different levels of English when they enter the class and may have studied in different places, using different methods, their knowledge will not always be the same. An element of grammatical revision, of remedial work, is essential. Each unit therefore contains a Checklist of grammatical items which must be thoroughly understood before students can expect to deal adequately with the composition topics at the end of the unit. It must be stressed that hardly any of the grammatical items should be new, so that students must judge, with the teacher's guidance, whether some remedial practice, using the exercises in *Book 3*, is necessary or not. The Checklist appears at the beginning of the unit, not at the end, precisely for this reason; it is not a summary of what has been taught in the unit, but a reminder of what students should already be familiar with, to enable them to use the structures themselves in the unit that follows.

Within each unit, we have tried to exemplify the kinds of composition students may be asked to write, we have provided indications of how they are put together, and we have offered students numerous opportunities to develop their own skills in activities which, while they are in principle designed for work in pairs or groups, can also, in almost every case, be done by individual students.

One final comment is required. Writing well in English is a matter of learning a number of skills and putting them into constant practice. The composition tasks at the end of each unit arise naturally out of the themes contained in it and necessarily demand confident handling of the structures emphasised. If there is one thing a further ten years' experience in teaching Cambridge classes has taught us, it is that students, and teachers, too, frequently underestimate the amount of work that can and should be done outside the classroom. It is vital for any student who hopes to pass the examination to find the time for written practice; it is also vital that students should make thorough use of the reference sections provided in the books in this course, whenever they are in doubt.

That said, I would like to add that we hope that the material and guidance given in this book are interesting enough for writing in English to become not a task, but an enjoyable experience.

Will Fowler
Barcelona, June 1983

● **Acknowledgements**

Thanks are due to the following for permission to reproduce copyright material:

Weidenfield & Nicholson Limited for an extract from *Evader* by T. D. G. Teare, published in *Great Escape Stories* edited by Dr Eric Williams; The Sunday Times for information given in two articles on the *Masquerade* treasure hunt of Kit Williams by Simon Freeman which appeared in the Sunday Times of 14 March 1982; Mitchell Beazley for the extracts on Keeping Fit and First Aid from the *Man and Society* volume of *The Mitchell Beazley Joy of Knowledge Library*.

The recipes for Hungarian Goulash and Moussaka are taken from *The Cookery Year*, © 1981/73 Reader's Digest Association Limited, London. Used with permission.

The publishers would also like to thank Pizza Express Ltd. for the use of their restaurant in Bridge Street, Walton-on-Thames in two photographs on page 99.

Thanks are due to the following for permission to reproduce photographs:

VRU (Thomas Nelson) pp. 2, 56, 83, 84, 99   Rex Features pp. 3, 6, 120   Barnaby's pp. 11, 39, 83, 133   Brian Shuel p. 39   BTA pp. 40, 41, 110   National Film Archive/Laser/I. Bergman p. 72   Anthony Blake pp. 76, 77   David Redfern p. 100 Radio Times Hulton Picture Library pp. 102, 103, 109   NFA/Rank/Jolly/Inter Mondia p. 105 NFA/20th Century Fox   p. 105   NFA/United Artists/Warners p. 105   NFA/UIP/Paramount p. 106   Science Photo Library p. 112 Observer/Kit Williams p. 135 NFA/Columbia/EMI/Warner p. 138

Every effort has been made to trace owners of copyright and if any omissions can be rectified the publishers will be pleased to make the necessary arrangements.

Description: People

Checklist

Each unit in this book shows you how to write a different kind of composition. Before you begin to study the text, however, it is a good idea to remind yourself of the forms and structures that are likely to be required in a given case. You will recognise almost all of them because you have learned them before, but it is useful 1) to look at the grammatical notes contained on the first page of the unit; 2) if you are still not sure, to do the relevant exercise indicated here in *New First Certificate English Book 3*; 3) when you are writing a composition, to check any point you are doubtful of in the Reference Section at the end of this book.

● **Tenses in future time**

I**'m going to** meet her at the airport. (Personal intention)
She **is coming** to see us today. (She has planned the visit.)
Her plane **arrives** at 11.30. (Planned according to a timetable)
I'm sure/I hope she**'ll** (she **will**) **be** there.
If you wait here, you**'ll see** her.
You**'ll see** her **when** she comes through the door.
When you see her, **tell** her I'm waiting for her at the office.

(**Will** is mainly used as the future form in subordinate clauses or in sentences with subordinate clauses (**if, when**) in the present tense. It may be replaced by the imperative.)

See Book 3, Exercises 96A—B.

Shall I meet her at the airport? = Would you like me to ...?
(**Shall** is only necessary as the future form when we are offering to do something or making a suggestion. It is used only with **I** and **we**, e.g. **Shall I ...? Shall we ...?**)

See Book 3, Exercise 28.

● **Tenses in past-to-present time**

I **have been studying** English **for** four years/since 19__ (up to now).
I **haven't seen** her **for** a long time/**since** last Christmas.
I **studied** French **for** five years at school (but I don't study it now).
I **started** learning English/**stopped** learning French four years **ago**.

See Book 3, Exercises 97A—C.

● **Describing appearance and dress**

She**'s** tall/short/**quite** slim/**rather** fat.
He **has** blue eyes. He**'s** a blue-eyed boy.
She**'s wearing** a red coat. She **has** a red coat **on**. She**'s dressed in** red.
He **has** a beard/a moustache. He**'s wearing** dark glasses.
A man **with** a beard/moustache. A man **in** dark glasses.
A man **in** a green jacket. **Put** your jacket **on**/**Take** it **off**.

1

1.1 Physical appearance

● **Dialogue 1** 🔲

Sandra Wyatt, Managing Director of Mediterranean Fashions, is talking to her secretary, June Taylor.

Listen to the dialogue.

SANDRA Now, as you know, June, Mrs Campesi is coming to see us today. She's flying from Rome and I'd like you to go and meet her at the airport. She'll probably expect to see me there, but I want to check a few details about the last delivery from Italy before she arrives.

JUNE She's an important supplier, isn't she? I've written a lot of letters to her. I hope I'll recognise her. What does she look like?

SANDRA She's quite tall, about the same height as you, and fair-haired. She has very striking green eyes, and a good figure. She's slim and she's always very well dressed.

JUNE How old is she?

SANDRA About 35, I suppose, but she looks younger and she usually wears young women's clothes.

JUNE Have you got a photograph of her?

SANDRA No, I'm afraid not. But I'm sure you'll recognise her. She looks very smart, like most Italian women.

JUNE What time shall I go to meet her, Mrs Wyatt?

SANDRA Her plane arrives at 11.30. You'll just have time to get to the airport. When you see her, tell her I'm sorry I couldn't come myself. I'll be here at the office.

● **Activity 1**

Look at the four photographs below and identify Mrs Campesi from Sandra's description. Give reasons for your choice.

● **Dialogue 2** 🔲

June is at the information desk at the airport.

Listen to the dialogue.

JUNE Has the Alitalia flight from Rome arrived yet?

CLERK Yes, it touched down ten minutes ago.

JUNE Oh, dear. I have to meet someone. I hope I haven't missed her.

CLERK Don't worry. The passengers are still going through customs. If you wait over there, you'll see them when they come through that door.

JUNE Thanks.

● **Activity 2**

Before you go on, decide what sort of person June is looking for. Describe the person she is expecting to see.

2

● Dialogue 3 🎙

Listen to the dialogue.

JUNE Hm, tall, fair-haired, with green eyes, looks about 30. Ah, that woman coming through now must be her! Oh, excuse me, are you Mrs Campesi?

WOMAN I'm sorry. I'm not. You've made a mistake, I'm afraid.

JUNE Sorry. Well, there isn't anyone here like Mrs Campesi. That woman in the bright blue coat waiting over there is tall and slim, but she's got red hair and she's wearing dark glasses. Oh, well, I'll ask her, anyway. Excuse me, I'm looking for Mrs Fulvia Campesi, from Rome.

MRS CAMPESI Ah, pleased to meet you. I'm Fulvia Campesi. I was expecting Mrs Wyatt but I couldn't see her so I waited for a few minutes.

JUNE I'm her secretary. She asked me to meet you. I'm sorry I didn't recognise you at first.

MRS CAMPESI Of course, I've got these dark glasses on. That makes it difficult.

JUNE Yes, and...er.

MRS CAMPESI Ah, and my hair, too. I expect I was fairer when I came before. Oh well, never mind. You found me in the end.

JUNE Yes. We can go this way to get a taxi. Can I help you with your luggage?

● Activity 3 — pair work

Describe the people in the photographs below. Compare your description with another student's.

● Activity 4 — group work

You work for an advertising company and must choose actors and actresses for some comic sketches advertising a new soft drink. Decide what you want them to look like and how you want them to be dressed. The sketches include a) a gangster and his girlfriend; b) Tarzan and Jane; c) Mark Antony and Cleopatra; d) a typical English businessman and his wife; e) King Arthur and his wife, Guinevere. Compare your descriptions with other students'.

1.2 Character, qualifications and experience

● **Applying for a job**

Study the form of address and the layout of the beginning and end of these letters, and look at Reference Section — Letters, page 161.

Administrative Assistant required for journal published by large charity organisation. 'A' levels, good typing (at least 45 w.p.m.) and a willingness to take responsibility essential. Apply in writing to: Mr S Heywood, Box 3939, Haymarket House, London SW1 3PQ.

Au pair wanted Jan.-Jul. by doctor's family in London, 2 young children. Write to: Dr and Mrs Watson, 64 Oakley Road, London SW2.

25th April 1984

28, Stanton Lane,
Hollington,
Yorkshire.

Dear Mr. Heywood,

REASON FOR WRITING

I am writing to apply for the post of Administrative Assistant, advertised in the 'Daily Star' yesterday, 24th April.

EXPERIENCE

I have no previous experience in charity work, but I have been working for a year in a youth centre in York. As part of my job here, I have had to help in the preparation of the club's monthly magazine. It is my responsibility to persuade the contributors to hand in their articles and illustrations on time, to deal with problems of layout, and to organise distribution.

QUALIFICATIONS

I have 'A' level passes in English, History and French and enclose a photocopy of the certificates. I can type 50 words a minute.

ENDING LETTER

I look forward to hearing from you.

Yours sincerely,

Anne Taylor

Anne Taylor

September 22, 1984

9 Rue de Breuil
75014 Paris
FRANCE

Dear Dr and Mrs Watson

REASON FOR WRITING

I am replying to your advertisement in 'The Lady' for an au pair to look after your children and help in the house from January to July next year.

QUALIFICATIONS

As you will see from the enclosed application form, I have just left school here, after completing my baccalaureat. I have been studying English for six years, but I would like to spend some time improving it by living in an English-speaking country before going to university next autumn.

EXPERIENCE

I am used to dealing with children because I have two brothers, one ten years old and the other eight and I have always done everything I can to help my mother, who has a full-time job. In addition, I have had a lot of experience in baby-sitting for couples in the neighbourhood, and as a result that I have learnt how to deal with most of the emergencies that occur when you have to look after children.

REQUESTING INFORMATION

I look forward to hearing from you about the job. In particular, I would like to know about the hours of work, the responsibilities I would have, and the opportunities I would have for study.

Yours sincerely

Francoise Deferre

Francoise Deferre

● Activity 5

Study the letters opposite and notice that they follow four basic stages:
1) reason for writing;
2) introducing yourself, and giving reason for application;
3) previous experience and qualifications;
4) polite ending, and possible request for further information.

Work together to write a letter to apply for one of the jobs below. First, decide what sort of person is likely to get the job — age, sex, previous experience, qualifications, etc. — and what else you would like to know about it if you applied. Then write the letter from an appropriate applicant. Remember to state:
1) how and where you saw the advertisement;
2) why you want the job;
3) your experience and qualifications;
4) any requests for further information.
End the letter correctly and lay it out like those on the opposite page.

FRENCH, SPANISH, GREEK, ITALIAN, GERMAN, PORTUGUESE . . . TRANSLATOR/WRITERS

European magazine is expanding its London staff. It requires experienced Translator/Writers, with any of the above languages as mother tongue, to take responsibility for separate-language editions of monthly journal. Previous magazine experience and good knowledge of European affairs essential. Salary negotiable. Application with full c.v. to Vittorio Moro, EUROPE TODAY, 707 Camden Road, LONDON W11.

HOUSEKEEPER USA

For New York-based executive with heavy travel schedule. Must be healthy woman under 25. Competent, with previous experience. Write to Edwin Flint, Jr. c/o George V Hotel, LONDON. Or come to interview on Tuesday October 22. Passport required.

BIOLOGY BOOKROOM

If you have an interest in biology, like to do things thoroughly, and don't mind dealing with the unexpected you may be the person we are looking for to join us as an assistant in our largely | mail order biological bookshop.

We offer a friendly atmosphere, a varied and often unpredictable working day, and a salary in the region of £5500.

Write with full curriculum vitae to Miss Linda Hayman, BGM Bookroom, 733 Bloomsbury Street, LONDON WC1B 4ZZ.

1.3 A life history

Jane Fonda

Actress daughter of the late Henry Fonda, she was born on December 21, 1937, in New Jersey, but brought up on the West Coast till she was ten. She was educated at the exclusive women's college, Vassar, but grew restless there and left to go and study art in Paris. When she returned to New York, she took up modelling and appeared twice on the cover of *Vogue.* In 1958 she met Lee Strasberg, founder of the Actors' Studio, and this led her to develop a passion for acting. In 1960 she made both her Broadway and Hollywood debuts, and won immediate recognition as a potential star.

In 1965 she married French director Roger Vadim, who tried to make her into another Bardot, but in the late 1960s she returned to the U.S. and became a fervent social activist, supporting anti-Establishment causes like the Black Panthers, the Indians, and the anti-Vietnam war movement. In 1969 she won her first nomination for an Oscar, and won the New York Film Critics' Award, for her performance in *They Shoot Horses, Don't They?* For *Klute,* in 1971, she won the Academy Award as best actress, as well as another New York Critics' Award.

In the late 1970s, after a period of being involved in anti-war activities with her second husband, Tom Hayden, she returned to participate in the commercial cinema. She won a nomination for an Academy Award as best actress in *Julia* (1977), and her second Oscar as best actress for *Coming Home* (1978), a film dealing with the aftermath of the Vietnam war.

● **Activity 6**

Using the notes below, write brief life histories of the following people.

GLENDA JACKSON
Born May 9, 1936
Place Birkenhead, U.K.
Father Bricklayer
Began acting 16, when left school
Jobs Waitress, receptionist, chemist's assistant
First big film success *Marat/Sade*
Awards Oscar for best actress, *Women in Love* (1969) and *A Touch of Class* (1973).

MELINA MERCOURI
Born October 10, 1923
Place Athens, Greece
Father Politician, once Deputy Mayor of Athens
Began acting 17
First film *Stella* (1955) directed by Cacoyannis (*Zorba*)
Awards Nominated for the Oscar for *Never on Sunday;* best actress at Cannes (1960).
Other Elected Member of Parliament for Piraeus (1977). Now Minister of Culture.

DUSTIN HOFFMAN
Born August 8, 1937
Place Los Angeles, U.S.A.
Father Furniture designer
Began acting 19
Jobs Doorkeeper in flats, attendant in mental hospital
First big film success *The Graduate* (1967)
Awards Nominated for Academy Award in *The Graduate*, *Midnight Cowboy*, *Lenny* and *Tootsie* (1967, 1969, 1974 and 1983). Oscar in 1980 for *Kramer v. Kramer.*

● **Composition**

1 Write an application for one of the jobs on page 5.
2 Write a brief biography of any famous person. Use the order of presentation given in Activity 6.
3 Describe the appearance of a friend of yours.

Making enquiries

Checklist

● **Direct and indirect questions**

In indirect questions, notice the order —
subject before verb — and the fact that **do**
and **does** do not appear in the Present Simple
tense.

'**Is there** a telephone box near your house?' —
Can you tell me **if there's** a telephone box near
your house? (No question word in the original
question)
'**Where's** the post office?' — Can you tell me
where the post office **is**?
'**How far is** the station from here?' — Can you
tell me **how far** the station **is** from here?
'**How often do** the buses **run**?' — I'd like to
know **how often** the buses **run**.
'**How long does it take** to get to the centre of
London?' — She wants to know **how long it
takes** to get to the centre of London.
'**How big is** the flat?' — The advertisement
doesn't say **how big** the flat **is**.

See Book 3, Exercise 1.

● **There is/are**

There is/are indicates the existence of
something. Do not confuse it with impersonal
forms, like **It's easy, It's a nice day today**.

Is there a garage at the hotel?
— Yes, **there is**. **There's** room for a hundred
cars.
Are there a lot of good hotels in Athens?
— Oh, **there are** several.

● **Polite requests**

Could I come round and have a look at the
flat?
Would you mind if I came round and had a
look at the flat?
Could you tell me something about the job I've
applied for?
**Would you tell me .../Would you mind telling
me ...?**

Study Reference Section — Modals, page 149.

● **Offers**

Would you like me to help you?/**Shall I** help
you?

Study Reference Section — Modals, page 149.

2.1 Telephone enquiries

N.W.10 SHORT LET 2 months Nov/Dec. Single/double bedroom or flat. Ring 403 0059.

NEWCROSS BROCKLEY Large room in shared flat £50 pcm. 694 8724.

3-BEDROOM HOUSE available November in Forest Hill. Full central heating, suit family or shares. References essential. £90 pw. Tel. Biggin Hill 46193.

GIRL WANTED for third person in shared house SE15. Garden, colour TV. £10pw. rent, £4 pw. bills. 639 5020 evenings/weekends.

PRIMROSE HILL flat. Suit 3 people. £140 pcm. Phone 873 7741.

MAIDA VALE Large 1-bed. flat £130 pcm inclusive. Available from Nov. 1st. Tel. 178 7451.

● Dialogue 1

Listen to the dialogue.

MRS TOWNSEND Hello, Eileen Townsend speaking.

SANDY Oh, hello. I'm ringing about the flat advertised in today's *Star*. Is it still available?

MRS T Yes, it is. Two or three people have rung up about it, but nobody's been to see it yet.

SANDY I see. It doesn't say how big it is in the advertisement.

MRS T Well, it's got two bedrooms, a double and a single, and there's a dining/living room, a fair-sized kitchen and a big bathroom. And there's garage space if you want it.

SANDY It certainly sounds nice. Could I come round and have a look at it sometime this morning?

MRS T Oh yes. Come any time you like. I'll be at home all day today and tomorrow...until the flat's let, I mean.

SANDY Oh good. Well, I'll come round as soon as I can. Could you give me the exact address, please?

MRS T It's 14, Primrose Crescent, Flat B.

SANDY (*noting it down*) 14, Primrose Crescent...Flat B. Thanks very much, Mrs Townsend. See you soon. 'Bye.

MRS T 'Bye. (*hangs up*)

● Activity 1 — pair work

Study the advertisement and the conversation above. Imagine Sandy likes the flat, but she wants to ask Mrs Townsend some questions. Ask and answer questions on the topics suggested below.

1	NEARBY FACILITIES		2	TRAVEL	
	supermarket	Is there...?		tube station	Is there...?
	shopping centre	Where...?		bus stop	Where...?
	post office	How far away...?		distance from	How far away...?
	cinema			London?	How often...?
	launderette				How long...take...?

3	FACILITIES IN FLAT		4	PAYMENT	
	telephone	Is there...?		rent	How much...?
	garage	How much extra...?		electric light	How often...?
	flats in building	How many...?		telephone	
	dog, cat	Can we...?			
	redecorating				

Secretary wanted for Japanese electronics company. Phone 285 4113.

● **Dialogue 2**

Listen to the dialogue.

FIONA Hello, Mitsuo Electronics. Can I help you?

SALLY Oh hello. I'm calling about the job advertised in this morning's *Standard*. Could you tell me some more about it, please?

FIONA Yes, of course. It's a secretarial job, at a fairly low level to start with, but Mitsuo's a very big company, so there are very good prospects for promotion if you like the work.

SALLY And what sort of qualifications do I need, exactly?

FIONA Well, good speeds in shorthand and typing, about 90 words a minute in shorthand and 45 in typing, a good telephone manner, and it would be an advantage if you could offer some experience with office computers and telex.

SALLY I've worked with telex, of course, but not with computers.

FIONA Oh, don't worry. If you're selected at the interview the company will send you on a training course anyway. We're holding interviews next Monday morning. Would you like me to put your name down?

SALLY Oh yes, I would. My name's Sally Tate, spelt T - A - T - E.

FIONA Right, good. 11.30 on Monday morning. Oh, by the way, the company pays your travel expenses, of course.

SALLY Oh...thanks. 'Bye, then.

FIONA 'Bye.

● **Activity 2 — pair work**

Study the conversation between Fiona and Sally. Sally gets the job as secretary to Mr Takahashi. When she arrives at work on the first day she asks Fiona some questions about the job and the company. Below are Fiona's answers. Form the questions and then say what Sally wants to know.

e.g. Oh, he's very considerate to his staff, but he sometimes asks them to work late.

SALLY What's Mr Takahashi like?

Sally wants to know what Mr Takahashi is like.

1 There are 27 Japanese working here.

2 You'll have to take shorthand, answer correspondence, type a report occasionally and make travel arrangements — that sort of thing.

3 Yes, it's open for lunch from 12.30-2.00.

4 The ladies' room on this floor is at the end of the corridor on the right.

5 Oh, you can take holidays whenever you like, provided you give Mr Takahashi enough notice.

6 You're supposed to report directly to Mr Takahashi, but you can always go to the personnel manager for advice.

7 You'll work alone. We don't have typing pools here.

8 We get paid on Friday mornings, unless you'd rather be paid monthly.

2.2 Travel enquiries

● Dialogue 3

In a travel agency. Ivor Jones, the travel
agent, gives Peggy Cripps some information
about holidays.

Listen to the dialogue.

IVOR Morning, madam. Can I help you?

PEGGY It's about these holidays in Greece that
you have advertised in this morning's paper.
Could you tell me some more about them,
please?

IVOR Of course. Do you mean the fortnight in
Athens, or the two-week tour of the islands?

PEGGY We were thinking of the fortnight based
in Athens.

IVOR Well, for £225 per head we include the
flight there and back, of course, and two weeks'
full board in a four-star hotel.

PEGGY Is anything else included?

IVOR Oh yes. As well as the return flight and
the hotel, we include two organised trips, one to
the islands, which lasts a full day, and the other
a half-day guided tour of Athens. And there's a
coach to meet you when you arrive at Athens
airport, and to take you there at the end of your
stay.

PEGGY And could we get to Delphi?

IVOR Yes. There's a full programme of optional
excursions to places like Delphi and Corinth,
and some longer ones to the islands. We charge
extra for those, of course, but I think you'll find
they're very reasonably priced.

PEGGY Could you give me some idea of how
much a typical day trip would cost? To Delphi,
for example.

IVOR To Delphi? Let me see. It's a day trip
with lunch and the guide included, and it costs
about £16 each.

PEGGY And what's the hotel like? What sort of
facilities does it offer?

IVOR Well, it's got a swimming pool, and
there's a hotel bus that takes you to the beach
in the morning and brings you back in the
afternoon. And in the hotel itself there are the
usual things, a disco, a bar and so on.

PEGGY That sounds good. Well, I'd like to talk
this over with my husband at lunchtime, and
I'll be back this afternoon if he agrees. What
time do you close?

IVOR At five o'clock, but I wouldn't leave it too
late if I were you, because there aren't many
places left. We wouldn't like you to be
disappointed.

BREAKAWAY IN WINTER

...to Warm Greece

It's never too late to catch the sunshine in the islands, or to see the sunset from the Acropolis. Superb value in this PANORAMA Special Winter Offer. For £225, 2 weeks bed-and-breakfast in 4-star Athens hotel with disco, bar and rooftop swimming pool, plus private beach with hotel transport laid on. Price also includes whole-day island trip and guided city tour. Optional full-day guided tours to Delphi, Corinth, etc at reasonable prices. (Allow £16 per trip.) Departures every Wednesday and Sunday throughout October and November.

● **Activity 3 — pair work**

Ivor gives Peggy the above brochure information. Peggy goes home to tell Jack, her husband, about the trip. She studies all the information so that she can answer his questions. Work in pairs, with one of you as Peggy and the other as Jack to work out their dialogue.

JACK	PEGGY
wants to know if Peggy went to the agency.	replies.
wants to know what is/was included in the £225.	replies from memory, forgetting something, but then remembers.
wants to know what sort of hotels they would stay in.	replies enthusiastically.
wants to know the distance of the hotels from the beach.	replies, making it sound attractive.
wants to know about any optional trips and their destinations.	replies enthusiastically.
wants to know if they can go on any longer trips.	replies in detail.
wants to know how to make bookings.	replies, exaggerating the urgency a little.
gives his opinion/decision.	

● **Activity 4 — role-play**

Work in groups of three. While on holiday in Athens, Peggy (or Jack) meets an old person. He/She is trying to explain to the receptionist at their hotel that he/she has lost a shoulder-bag, perhaps in the hotel bus, but is nervous and confused. Peggy (Jack) helps.
Before beginning the role-play:
1) the tourist must prepare a description of the bag and its contents;
2) the receptionist must think of questions: — she wants to know the colour and size of the bag, what it was made of, where it was lost, where the person was sitting in the bus, if there was anything valuable in it, etc.;
3) Peggy/Jack acts as interpreter, repeating the questions and answers: **He/she wants to know... He/she says...**

2.3 Choosing your holiday

INDIA

In 12 remarkable days see the HIGHLIGHTS OF INDIA —Delhi, Agra and Jaipur from only £775, frequent departures. In 18 days see India and Nepal with time to relax and enjoy a stay in Goa, with its fine beaches —£1425, depart December 18. For those who marvel at the magnificence of the Himalayas, our 19-day journey through India visits Delhi, Jaipur, Agra, Kathmandu, Sikkim, Darjeeling and finally Kashmir, for a relaxing stay on a beautiful houseboat—£1495, depart 5 January.

£775

NILE CRUISES

See the splendour of Egypt and the Nile, the Pyramids and Sphinx at Giza and the Tombs of the Pharaohs at Luxor; and then cruise from Luxor to Aswan, visiting ancient temples along this historic river. Full board, 15 days. Escorted. Departures from December to May. Or . . . 8 days in Cairo with weekend visit to Aswan and Luxor from £550.

£1200

ski
WITHOUT GOING BROKE!
9 days in the French Alps
from only **£127**

9 days in the French Alps **from only £127!** Les Arcs, Puy Saint Vincent and introducing Risoul. 7 full days of skiing. Direct coach travel London to resort. Self-catering apartments right on the slopes.
NEW Holidays by jet to Avoriaz from £99.
NEW Try our 'Alpine Rendezvous'—two weeks demi-pension (half-board for us) at Puy Saint Vincent from £185.

● **Activity 5 — role-play**

Work in groups of four. One of you is the travel agent, each of the others asks him/her questions about one of the holidays in the advertisements above. The travel agent gives them the information.

● **Composition**

1 Some friends of yours abroad have seen an advertisement for a beach-side flat near your town, and have asked you to check that it is as good as the advertisement says You have seen the agent for the flat. Write to your friends, reporting what he/she told you.

2 Write a letter from Sandy to her parents (see page 8) telling them that she has rented a flat from Mrs Townsend and describing it.

3 Write a letter from Sally to a friend (see page 9) describing her first day at the office.

Discussion: Making comparisons

Checklist

Sooner or later, almost every discussion involves making comparisons. Study the examples carefully to remind yourself of the main forms.

● **Comparison: regular forms**

We need a **more responsible** person, with a **stronger** personality.

Study Reference Section — Adjectives, page 145, for advice on the correct forms for one-, two- and three-syllable adjectives.

He is **much** (far) **older** and **far** (much) **more experienced than** the others. (Making a comparison, but emphasising the difference)
She writes **more neatly than** he does. (adverbial)
She is **the youngest** candidate, but she has **the most attractive** personality.
She is one of **the neatest/the most efficient** people in the world.

● **Comparison: irregular forms**

She has **more/less** experience **than** the other candidates.
He has**n't as much** experience as the others (have).
She has **better** qualifications (than he has).
His qualifications are not **as good as** hers.

much/many, **more**, (the) **most**
good, **better**, (the) **best**
little/few, **less/fewer**, (the) **least/fewest**
bad, **worse**, (the) **worst**

● **Other forms of comparison**

He is **as** responsible **as** his sister, but **not as/so** tidy.
I have **the same** problems **as** they have.
Her attitude is **similar to** mine/**like** mine.
His qualifications are **different from** mine/**not the same as** mine.

See Book 3, Exercises 3A—D.

● **Too and enough**

Note the word order with **enough**: with nouns (before) and adjectives and adverbs (after).
Note the use of **too** (NOT 'too much') with adjectives and adverbs.

This flat is **too** expensive/**not** cheap **enough** for us.
We haven**'t** got **enough** money (to pay for it).
He dresses **too** casually.
He doesn**'t** dress smartly **enough**.

See Book 3, Exercises 33A—B .

3.1 Choosing a flat

● **Dialogue 1**

Odette and Giovanna are language students in Oxford who want to rent a flat with two other friends.

Listen to the dialogue.

ODETTE Well, what sort of a place are we looking for?

GIOVANNA Somewhere...somewhere nice and cheap, and nearer the town centre than this residence.

ODETTE And not too expensive. Don't let's forget that!

GIOVANNA Right. How much can we afford?

ODETTE I'd say not more than £15 each a week, at the most!

GIOVANNA Oh, not so much as that! Can't we find anything cheaper?

ODETTE All right, Giovanna. Why not just start reading them out? Just those that are cheaper than £60 a week, but not too far away.

GIOVANNA There's one here, in St John Street. £60 a week, exactly.

ODETTE No, we haven't really got enough money. Aren't there any cheaper ones?

GIOVANNA Norham Gardens. 8 minutes from the centre. That's quite close.

ODETTE Yes, that's near enough to the centre, and to the school. And how many rooms has it got? Don't forget we're going to share with Pilar and Sofia.

GIOVANNA Two. Not as many as the one in St John Street. But we could share, if they're big enough.

ODETTE That one may be worth looking at.

GIOVANNA O.K., I've put a mark against it. How about this? Headington Hill. Five minutes by bus to the centre. Two rooms, but it's less expensive.

ODETTE But it's much further out.

GIOVANNA Headington? Oh yes, that's too far. That's miles out!

ODETTE The best one so far was the one in Norham Gardens.

GIOVANNA But it's only got two rooms. It may be too small.

ODETTE Oh well, let's carry on looking then. What's the next, Giovanna?

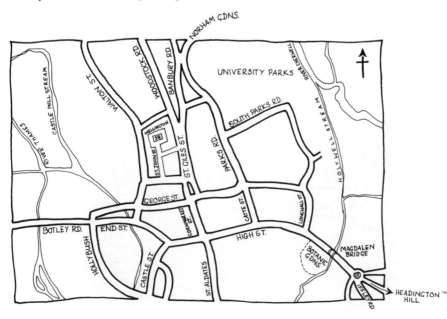

14

● Activity 1

Abbreviations are often used in accommodation advertisements. Look at the following list of abbreviations and match each with its appropriate full form on the right.

Abbreviation	Full form
lge	central heating
p.w.	telephone
lux.flt.	bedsitter
gge.	colour TV
c.h.	per week
hse.	sharing
tel.	bathroom with WC
bedsit.	rooms
col.TV	garage
rms.	large
sh.	house
b/WC	luxury flat
gdn.	references
evngs.	electricity & gas included
c.h.w.	separate
bed.	evenings
furn.	minutes
refs.	garden
elec. & gas inc.	furnished
1st fl.	kitchen and bathroom
min.	modern
s/c	constant hot water
sep.	bedrooms
mod.	self-contained
k/b	first floor

● Activity 2 — group work

Work in groups of four. You are language students in Oxford and you want to rent a flat on a shared basis, with your own rooms if possible. You can afford about £48 per week altogether and you want a place quite near your language school in central Oxford. Look at this list of advertisements from the local newspaper. Make a short list of three possibilities, giving reasons for your preferences and say why you reject the others.

139 St John Street. 5 min. centre. s/c c.h. fully furn. 3-rm. 2nd fl. flt. b/WC. refs. £60 p.w. 85472 after 6 p.m.

165 Norham Gdns. 8 min. centre. mod. s/c furn. flt. 2 rms. k/b & 2nd WC. elec. & gas inc. £46 p.w. 89148 before 9 a.m. or after 5:45 p.m.

229 Headington Hill. 5 min. bus to centre. s/c c.h. 3rd fl. flt. 2 rms. k/b tel. refs. £44 p.w. 95947, evngs.

257 Iffley Rd. bedsit. sh. k/b. 2nd fl. suit 2 sh. £30. 85792.

357 Cowley Rd. 15 min. bus to centre. s/c c.h. 1st fl. flt. c.h.w. 3 rms. k/b. gdn. refs. £44. 90371 evngs.

133 St Margaret's Rd. 10 min. centre. s/c furn. flt. 4 rms. lge. k/b. col. TV. suit 4 sh. £52. 91072 after 6 p.m.

177 Walton St. 5 min. centre. s/c furn. flt. 2nd fl. 3 rms. c.h.w. c.h. tel. elec. & gas inc. £48. 96954 after 4 p.m.

203 Bardwell Road. furn. hse. 6 rms. k/2b. 2 sep WC. col. TV. gdn. gge. £115 p.w. 91542 after 5 p.m.

122 Turl St. nr market. s/c c.h. flt. above shop. v. central. 2 rms. k/b. elec. & gas inc. £45 p.w. 97373.

10 Park Town. 10 min. centre. s/c. c.h. tel. 4 rms. lge. gge. k/2b. col. TV. gdn. £75. refs. Call 98989 any time to fix visit.

3.2 Comparing candidates

● **Activity 3**

There were over fifty applications for the job advertised here. The company made a short list of four candidates after the preliminary interview. In the final interview, however, none of the four came up to the standard required. Read these reports on the short-listed candidates and decide why they did not get the job.

WANTED URGENTLY

Courier/guide for International Coach Line. Must speak good French and either German or Italian, have a strong adaptable extrovert personality, like travel, be prepared to work long hours, and have ability to keep people's spirits up on long journeys.
Single people preferred.
Apply Box 7963.

NIKKI WATSON

Ms Watson seemed quite promising on paper and made a good impression at both interviews. She has travelled more than the other candidates and has far more experience of our routes than they have, but her knowledge of French and German is not as good as we would like and she has done almost all her travelling with friends. We are looking for a more responsible person, with greater experience with groups of people than Ms Watson, and a stronger personality.

PAUL ELLIOTT

Mr Elliott is much older than the others and far more experienced. He had the best qualifications of the four but turned out to be the most unsuitable for the job, in our opinion. He is clearly not patient or tolerant enough to deal with passengers. The worst thing about him at the interview was his manner; he was the most aggressive candidate we have ever met. We obviously require someone more tactful for this job, and less like a sergeant-major.

STEPHEN BOXER

Mr Boxer, the youngest candidate, has the most attractive personality of the four. He has not had as much experience as Ms Watson or Mr Elliott but is clearly much better at dealing with people. If he could learn to dress as well as he speaks, he would be suitable, but he made a bad impression at both interviews by turning up in the oldest, dirtiest pair of jeans we have ever seen. We may be stricter than other companies in demanding a high standard of personal appearance but believe Mr Boxer's attitude towards dress is too unconventional for this job.

JANET CARR

Ms Carr is the least experienced candidate. Her background is different from that of the others because she is a secretary in a travel agency. Her main weakness, however, is that her attitude to passengers would be similar to Mr Elliot's. No doubt she is one of the most efficient people in the world but she showed the same lack of understanding of passengers and their problems as he did.

Background information

In fact the coach line operates routes from London to Athens via Paris, Lyons, Milan, Trieste, Belgrade and Sofia. It caters for tourists (usually young working people or students) and for people on the route who use it for cheap inter-city travel. The company expects its couriers to dress neatly and look presentable (though there is no uniform), take an active interest in the passengers' welfare, work hard, etc., but pays them well. (Basic salary in the region of £7000 a year, depending on the number of trips made.)

● **Dialogue 2** 🎞

The International Coach Line readvertised the courier job after they found the first group of candidates unsuitable. Here is how the interviewers, Sally Phipps and Frank Green, began the interview with Martin Powell, one of the new group of possible candidates for the job.

Listen to the dialogue.

SALLY Come in, Mr Powell.

MARTIN Thank you.

FRANK Sit down, please.

SALLY Well, Mr Powell, we've got the information from your first interview here, and there are just a few more questions we'd like to ask. First, I see here that you've hitch-hiked all round Europe, but have you ever been to Greece?

MARTIN Oh yes, I've been several times. Three or four times to Athens and the mainland, and twice to the islands.

FRANK Did you go there by road? To Athens, I mean. Not the islands, of course!

MARTIN Yes. I hitched to Brindisi and then got the ferry to Patras and hitched from there into Athens.

SALLY Ah, so you've never been through Yugoslavia and Bulgaria?

MARTIN Well. I have visited Yugoslavia. I was in Dubrovnik for a week on a package tour. So I do know what it's like.

FRANK Yes, but it's one thing to visit a place alone, and another to be there with a coachload of tourists, you know.

MARTIN Oh, I think I'd be able to deal with that all right. I've been in a lot of difficult situations in my life, and I've always managed to find a way out.

SALLY But have you ever been in a group where people got lost, for example?

MARTIN Oh yes. Three times.

FRANK And where was that? What happened?...

NAME: Martin Powell AGE: 23 MARITAL STATUS: Single
EDUCATION: B.A. French and German

PRESENT JOB: Teacher.
REASON FOR LEAVING: Wants to see more of world, meet people and travel.
OTHER JOB EXPERIENCE: Barman. Hotel porter.

OTHER RELEVANT EXPERIENCE: 4 years as Boy Scout leader
TRAVEL: Has hitch-hiked widely in Europe. Knows Greece quite well.

LANGUAGES: Good French and German.
GENERAL IMPRESSION: Pleasant manner, good sense of humour, but rather inexperienced.

NAME: Tim Roach AGE: 49 MARITAL STATUS: Single
EDUCATION: Left school aged 15. Has navy certificates.

PRESENT JOB: Merchant Navy (25 years) Second mate.
REASON FOR LEAVING: Wants to leave sea, but keep on travelling.
OTHER JOB EXPERIENCE: Bricklayer. Delivery-van driver.

OTHER RELEVANT EXPERIENCE: Has sometimes helped courier friends.
TRAVEL: All over the world by sea, but less on land.

LANGUAGES: Quite good French. Some Italian and Greek.
GENERAL IMPRESSION: Cheerful personality, but rather impatient and insensitive.

NAME: Lynn Gillespie AGE: 17 MARITAL STATUS: Single
EDUCATION: Left school at 16. Has secreterial training.

PRESENT JOB: Hotel receptionist.
REASON FOR LEAVING: Wants to go back to Mediterranean, enjoys organising group activities.
OTHER JOB EXPERIENCE: None.

OTHER RELEVANT EXPERIENCE: Youth group leader. Plays guitar. Has organised several group excursions.
TRAVEL: Born and brought up in Italy for first 7 years (English parents). Has also lived in Greece (2 years).

LANGUAGES: Good Greek, some Italian and French.
GENERAL IMPRESSION: Hard-working, pleasant manner, but rather immature.

NAME: Liz Parker AGE: 33 MARITAL STATUS: Divorced
EDUCATION: Left school at 16. Qualified nurse.

PRESENT JOB: Sister in local hospital.
REASON FOR LEAVING: Would like to combine travelling with helping others. Needs change.
OTHER JOB EXPERIENCE: Shop assistant.

OTHER RELEVANT EXPERIENCE: Has organised trips for old people in U.K.
TRAVEL: Has made frequent coach trips to Spain, Italy and Greece.

LANGUAGES: Some French and Italian.
GENERAL IMPRESSION: Enthusiastic, adaptable, but rather bossy.

● Activity 4 — role-play

Divide into groups of six, two interviewers and four candidates. The interviewers must study the notes above about all four candidates. They must prepare the questions they are going to ask each one, including some to test the candidates' weaknesses. The four candidates must study only their own roles and prepare convincing answers on each point. When everyone is ready, the interviewers call each of the candidates one by one and take notes during the interviews. At the end, they must announce their decision and give their reasons for the choice.

● Composition

1 Would you rather live in a house or a flat? Give your reasons.
2 Write a report, based on Activity 4, saying why the interviewers in your group chose the successful candidate and not the others.
3 Who is the best driver or sportsman/ sportswoman or actor/actress you know or have seen? What makes this person better than others?

Invitations and replies

4

Checklist

● **Formulae for invitations**

Can you/Would you like to ...?
— Yes, **I'd love to/I'd be glad to** ...
— No, **I'm sorry, I can't, because** ...
— No, **I'd love to, but** ..., **because** ...

● **Word order of adverbs of frequency**

The main rule to follow is this: 1) after **to be**; 2) before the main verb; 3) between two auxiliaries.

He is **always** late. (After **to be**)
He **always** arrives late. (Before the main verb)
I have **often** told him about it. (After auxiliary, before the main verb)
We are **always** told to tell the truth. (Passive, after **to be**, before the main verb)
I would **never** have believed it if you hadn't told me. (Between two auxiliaries)

See Book 3, Exercise 5.

● **May (possibility)**

He **may arrive** late. (Perhaps he will ...)
You **may not remember** me, but we were at school together. (Perhaps you don't ...)
You **may not recognise** me when we meet again. (Perhaps you won't ...)
You **may have heard** about the accident. (Perhaps you have heard .../perhaps you heard ...)

Study Reference Section — Modals, page 149.

See Book 3, Exercise 35.

● **Exclamations**

How is used with adjectives; **what/what a** with nouns and with nouns preceded by adjectives.

What a pity (you can't come)! = It's such a pity you can't come.
How annoying (it/he is)! = It's/He's so annoying!
What a wonderful idea! = It's such a wonderful idea!
What nonsense! (Uncountable noun) = It's such nonsense!

See Book 3, Exercise 36.

● **Possessives**

A friend of **mine** = One of **my** friends
A friend of **my sister's** = One of **my sister's** friends
A friend of **Mr Smith's** = One of **Mr Smith's** friends

Note that we do NOT say 'a friend of me', so we do NOT say 'a friend of my sister' or 'a friend of Mr Smith'.

4.1 Spoken invitations

● **Dialogues 1 — 2** 📼

Maureen and Jill are having a party on Saturday. Maureen is ringing to invite two of her friends.

Listen to these two dialogues.

Dialogue 1 — acceptance

RUTH Hello. 743 7974.

MAUREEN Oh, hello. Is that you, Ruth? This is Maureen.

RUTH Hello, Maureen. How are you?

MAUREEN Fine, thanks. Listen! Jill and I are having a party on Saturday evening. Can you come?

RUTH Yes, I'd love to. What time?

MAUREEN Oh, any time after eight. Would your new room-mate like to come, too, do you think?

RUTH Jennie? Oh, yes, I'm sure she would — if she's not going out with her boyfriend, that is.

MAUREEN That's all right. She can bring him, too.

RUTH OK. I'll tell her. Would you like us to bring anything — a bottle or something?

MAUREEN No, Jill's looking after all that, and I'm doing the food.

RUTH Oh, well, fine. Thanks for ringing, and thanks for the invitation! I'm looking forward to the party.

MAUREEN See you on Saturday, then. 'Bye.

Dialogue 2 — polite refusal

CATHY Hello. Cathy Saunders speaking.

MAUREEN Oh, hello, Cathy. It's Maureen here. Jill and I are having a party on Saturday, and we hope you can come.

CATHY Oh, dear. This Saturday? How annoying! My mum and dad are going out so I suppose I'll have to look after my brother and sister.

MAUREEN Can't you get out of it?

CATHY I don't think so. I'm very sorry, Maureen. I really would like to come, but I don't see how I can fix it.

MAUREEN What a shame! Trevor will be disappointed.

CATHY Is Trevor coming? Oh!

MAUREEN Yes. As a matter of fact, he asked me if you'd be there...

CATHY Did he? You're not making it up, are you, Maureen? Look, I'll talk to my mum. Will it be all right if I ring you back tomorrow and let you know then?

MAUREEN Of course. And if I see Trevor, I'll tell him you're coming!

● **Activity 1**

Study these dialogues. Point out the words or phrases that indicate:
1) the invitation.
2) the acceptance or refusal and excuse.
3) an offer to help the person giving the party in the first dialogue.
4) an attempt to persuade Cathy to change her mind in the second dialogue.

● Activity 2 — role-play

Form groups of three for this exercise. In each of the situations below, one person, A, invites the other two, B and C, to do something; B accepts the invitation, but C refuses because he/she already has something else to do. Take it in turns to play A, B and C.

SITUATION 1

A has a house in the country, and B and C have never been there. A telephones to invite them for the weekend.

Preparation for the role-play

Person A
Decide:
1) where your country house is.
2) how far away it is from where you all live.
3) how you are all going to get there.
4) when the others should leave home.
5) when you are all coming back.

Person B
Think of questions you will need to ask A to find out more details about the weekend.

Person C
Like B, think of questions you will need to ask A, and also think of some reasons why you cannot accept the invitation.
e.g. Is the date inconvenient?
     Must you be at home this weekend? Why?
     What else have you got to do?
     Can you change your plans?

During the role–play

Person A — First invite B, then C to stay at your country house. When C refuses, try to persuade him/her.

Person B — Ask A questions to find out the answers to points 1-5 above. When you have the answers, accept the invitation.

Person C — Try to find out the answers to points 1-5 above, like B, but eventually refuse the invitation and make an excuse.

SITUATION 2

A wants to play tennis on Saturday afternoon. He/She has already found one person to play with, D, but would rather play doubles.

Preparation for the role-play

Person A
Decide:
1) where you are playing.
2) what time.
3) how you are going to get there.
4) who has already agreed to play.
5) if D plays well or not.

Person B
Think of questions you will need to ask A about arrangements for the game.

Person C
Think of questions to ask A, and decide why you cannot accept.
e.g. Are you doing something else?
     Are you injured and cannot play?
     Are the others too good?
     Can you change your plans?

During the role-play

Person A — First invite B, then C. When C refuses, try to persuade him/her to play, e.g. without C, there will be only three players.

Person B — Ask A questions about points 1-5 above, then accept the invitation.

Person C — Ask A questions about 1-5 above, but then give an excuse for refusing to play.

SITUATION 3

A would like to spend a fortnight's holiday abroad next summer, and invites B and C to go to Italy with him/her. Role-play the conversations in the same way, after deciding what questions will be necessary, and why C may refuse.

4.2 Written invitations

Study Sheila's letter below, then go on to do the exercises given for each of the following three letters.

36 Trelawny Gardens
London W6 7HP

14th April 1984

Dear Jane

CONTACT

You may not remember me after twenty years. It's a long time, isn't it? But I certainly remember you; and, like me, I am sure you have happy memories of the years when we were at school together. I especially remember that marvellous final year, when Stephen Simpson was our form master.

REASON FOR LETTER

Since leaving school, of course, we have all gone our different ways, but a few of us have kept in touch and we have often thought it would be a good idea to meet again and talk about old times. Now an ideal opportunity has occurred for a reunion. This July, it will be twenty years since we left school and, as you may have heard, Stephen Simpson is retiring.

INVITATION

Oliver Tripp, Peter Williams and I have formed a committee to organise a reunion dinner in London on the last Saturday in July. We are inviting Stephen as a guest of honour. We very much hope you can come.

REQUEST

We obtained your address from the school records, which may be out of date. However, if you have received this letter, we assume they are correct. If you are still in touch with any of our old classmates, it would be very helpful if you could let us have the latest addresses you have for them when you reply. We want to make sure of contacting everyone.

ENDING LETTER

We will let you have more details about the dinner when we have a clearer idea of how many people are coming. We look forward to hearing from you. Please reply to me at the above address.

Yours

Sheila Starling

Sheila Starling

---

18 Oak Court
Sanderscombe
Surrey   CR2 5PL

27th April 1984

Dear Sheila

It was a great pleasure to hear from you after such a long time, and I'm delighted that we'll have the chance of meeting again. The idea of a reunion dinner sounds wonderful and you can certainly count on me. As you can see, I still live quite near London so I'm sure I'll be able to come.

I'm looking forward to seeing you very much and naturally I'm curious to know how everyone is and, indeed, what they all look like after twenty years! We may not even recognise each other! Perhaps we ought to wear some kind of badge or label, or something. Seriously, though, I'm sure the reunion will be a great success and, as you say, it is particularly appropriate this year in view of Stephen Simpson's retirement. He was always so kind and understanding and I know we all owe him a great deal.

The only classmate I still keep in touch with is Christine Chapman. She moved down to the South Coast about a year ago, and the school may not have her new address, so I am enclosing it with this letter.

Kindest regards to Oliver and Peter.

Love,

Jane Prince

Jane Prince

Jane answers each part of Sheila's letter, but not always in the same order. Find the sentences or phrases where she
a) re-establishes friendly contact,
b) acknowledges the letter, c) accepts the invitation, d) answers Sheila's request.

Answer the following questions on Jim's letter to Sheila.
1 Why hasn't Jim replied to her letter before?
2 Would he like to come to the reunion?
3 Why must he refuse?
4 How does he re-establish friendly contact?
5 Can he help Sheila, or would he like her to help him? In what way?

132 Bridge Drive
Sydney
New South Wales
Australia

17 June 1984

Dear Sheila

As you will imagine, seeing my address, your letter took rather a long time to get to me. It was forwarded by the people who are now living in my old house in England. Unfortunately, the distance involved will also make it impossible for me to join you at your reunion dinner next month. I'm very sorry to miss it, because I would have enjoyed meeting you all again. Under the circumstances, I can only wish you a very happy evening together. Please give my kindest regards to everyone, and in particular, my best wishes to Stephen Simpson on his retirement.

I have been living out here for six years now. I have a good job and enjoy the climate here, though I think it will still be a few years before the neighbours accept my wife and me as Australians. We are still referred to as 'those Pommies'. Next year, I'm hoping to have a long holiday in Europe, however. I'd be grateful if you could send me the addresses of those who come to the dinner because I'd like to look up my old friends while I'm in England.

Once again with best wishes to everyone,

Yours

Jim Webster

Jim Webster

14 Langley Road
Liverpool

29th April 1984

Dear Sheila

1 Unfortunately, I am not sure whether I will be able to come. Rick (that's my husband) and I have planned to go to Switzerland for a holiday in July and I don't know if we will be back by the date you suggest. I would be very sorry to miss the reunion so I have asked Rick if we can leave for Switzerland a week earlier, but he says this may be difficult.

2 If I can come, I'll let you know straightaway, but if you don't hear from me, please give my best wishes to everyone, above all to Stephen Simpson. Hoping all the same to see you soon.

3 It was lovely to hear from you, especially in view of the reason for your letter. I have often thought that it is such a pity we seldom have the opportunity of meeting friends we made at school, and I think it is a wonderful idea of yours to organise this reunion.

4 I enclose the address of two people who were in our class, Julian Myers and Angela Lane. They got married a few years ago, and live near us. If I cannot come to the reunion after all, I would be very grateful if you could send me a list of those who came, with their addresses. I would like to know how everyone is getting on.

Sincerely

Margaret Wells

Margaret Wells

The four paragraphs in Margaret's reply to Sheila's letter are out of order. Put them in the right order and give reasons for your decision.

4.3 Making convincing excuses

Are you good at making excuses?

We are always told to tell the truth, but in some situations this may sound rude to the other person, or be annoying to ourselves. If you are going to tell lies, however, or invent excuses, they must be convincing.

Imagine you are in one of the following awkward situations, where you can either tell the unpleasant truth or say something that is not true. Remember that an unconvincing lie will be worse than the truth. Choose a), b) or c).

1 **Your boyfriend/girlfriend asks: Who were you talking to outside the cinema for such a long time last night? You reply:**
  a) Oh, I don't know. Some boy/girl who asked me the way to the station.
  b) A friend of my sister's. He/she wanted me to give Joan a message.
  c) That was Alan/Sarah. We were making a date for Saturday.

2 A friend who is proud of his boring home movies says: **Would you like to come to dinner on Wednesday night? Afterwards, we'll show you all our holiday pictures.** You say:
  a) Well, we wouldn't mind coming to dinner, but I don't think we could stand any more of your holiday films.
  b) We'd love to but we'll have to leave early, I'm afraid. I'm expecting an important call from Australia about 10:00.
  c) Oh, dear! Mary always goes to art classes on Wednesdays.

3 **The father of a friend of yours who thinks he looks like Paul Newman asks you: How old do you think I am? You say:**
  a) About 60.
  b) Not a day over 40.
  c) I really can't say, but of course you don't look old enough to be Anne's father.

4 You want to get home a bit early one evening because you are going out. The boss catches you leaving the office early, and asks why you are going home. You say:
  a) Actually, I'm going to the caterers to make sure of the arrangements for the office party tomorrow.
  b) Well, I'm going to a party tonight and I have to go home first to change.
  c) I've just had a phone call. My dear Aunt Lucy isn't feeling well.

5 **The self-important father of a friend of yours asks: Have I ever told you about the time when I was introduced to the Queen? You say:**
  a) No.
  b) Yes, frequently.
  c) Yes, I think you did. It must have been a wonderful experience.

● Composition

1 Someone you know tells you that an old friend you have not seen for a long time is going to be in your town soon, and gives you his/her address. Write and invite the friend to your house.

2 You have received an invitation to stay with a friend in the country for the weekend. Write, explaining that you cannot accept and suggest alternative dates.

3 You have received a formal invitation to a wedding 200 miles away. Write to the bride's parents, accepting but inquiring politely if they can advise you about staying the night nearby.

Narrative: Chronological sequence

Checklist

Telling a story in the Past tense can require various combinations of tenses. Study the examples below carefully.

● Chronological order (Past Simple and Continuous)

I **got up, shaved** and **had** breakfast. (Three consecutive actions, one after the other — Past Simple tense)
While I **was shaving**, I **was thinking** of the problems at work. (Two actions continuing for a period of time at the same time — Past Continuous tense)
While I **was having** breakfast, the telephone **rang**. (The second action took place in the middle of the first — Past Continuous for the first, because he/she continued to have breakfast afterwards, Past Simple for the second.)

● Previous action (Past Perfect)

It was the boss on the phone. He **wanted** to talk about the contract we **had signed** the previous day. (The main action, Past Simple — or Past Continuous in some cases — refers to something that had happened before, Past Perfect.)
He **said**, 'The other company **have changed** their minds'. (Direct speech)
He **told me that** the other company **had changed** their minds. (Indirect speech, requiring Past Perfect tense)

● Future reference in the past (would)

I **realised** that the other company **would want** to change the contract. = I thought, 'The other company will want to change the contract.' (Past Simple tense and **would** for the future reference)

I **asked** the boss if he **would need** my help. = I said, 'Will you need my help?' (Past Simple and **would**)

See Book 3, Exercises 96A, 97D—E.

● Verbs of perception and infinitive/-ing

Verbs of perception are frequently needed to describe past actions. Compare the use of the infinitive and **-ing** form after them.

I **heard** her **scream**. (Infinitive — she screamed once.)
I **heard** someone **calling** for help. (**-ing** form — the person called out several times.)
I **saw** him **raise** his hand. (A single, completed action — infinitive.)
I **saw** the river **flowing** under the bridge. (Rivers flow continuously — **-ing** form.)

See Book 3, Exercise 7.

5.1 Unusual events

There was a fire in the flat above ours last Monday evening. We were in the living-room — Joan was watching television and I was reading a book — when we suddenly heard a loud bang. I imagined that the old lady upstairs was moving the furniture about, and Joan was frightened that the noise would wake the baby. She turned down the television and a moment later we heard someone calling for help.

I ran upstairs. The old lady's door was shut but I could see smoke coming through the letter-box and under the door and could smell something burning. 'The flat's on fire!' I shouted down to Joan. 'Ring the fire brigade.'

I banged on the door but the old lady took a long time to answer. When she finally appeared, she said, 'I was having a bath when the water heater in the kitchen blew up.'

'Why didn't you open the door?' I asked her.

'I was getting dressed when you knocked,' she said, looking embarrassed.

I took her downstairs to our flat. Then I ran back, went inside her flat and turned the gas off to prevent another explosion. Smoke was pouring out of the kitchen and the heater was in flames. Just then I heard a fire engine arriving outside and the heavy footsteps of the firemen on the stairs. I looked round and noticed two of them standing in the doorway.

I left everything to them and went back to our flat. Joan was making the old lady a cup of tea. Soon afterwards, the fire chief came in to ask some questions. It turned out that the fire was not very serious, and the firemen were already putting it out. Joan went up with the old lady afterwards to help her clear up the mess.

When she came back, she said, 'It's all right now. Nothing was damaged except the heater. But wasn't it lucky that Timmy slept through all that noise?'

She took the teacups into the kitchen and I heard her scream and the cups crash to the floor. When I got there, water was dripping slowly from the ceiling and forming a pool on the floor. The baby woke up at last and started to cry.

● Activity 1

Make a list of all the actions in this story in chronological order (i.e. the order in which they happened) to construct the sequence of events. List actions that were taking place at the same time as others, and also actions that interrupted these continuing events. Did the interruption change the sequence? In other words, did the characters continue with the same action after the interruption?

Farley Fire Brigade was called out late on Monday evening to deal with a fire at 6 Burghill Court, Farley Hill, the home of Miss Elizabeth West, 73. The fire started when the water heater in Miss West's kitchen exploded while she was having a bath.

Firemen were quickly on the scene to put out the blaze, thanks to the prompt action of a young couple living in the flat downstairs, Mr and Mrs Handley. Mrs Handley dialled '999' while her husband rescued Miss West and turned off the gas to prevent a further explosion.

Superintendent Alan Blockley of the fire brigade told our reporter that no serious damage had been done. This was largely due to Mr and Mrs Handley, whose speed in contacting the fire brigade had prevented the fire from spreading to other houses in the neighbourhood.

● **Activity 2 — pair work**

Compare the newspaper report above with the narrative on page 26. The reporter is only interested in the main events, not in all the details. Find the main events in the original narrative. Has the order changed at all? Does the report refer back to previous actions anywhere? Does he mention anything that is not in the original story?

● **Activity 3 — group work**

Tell the following stories exactly according to the order of events.

STORY 1

BRIAN, 36. His wife, **ELSIE**, 32. Their son, **PAUL**, 9. **MRS CALDWELL**, 74, a neighbour. Mrs Caldwell's cat, **MOGGY**. You are **BRIAN**. Moggy on Mrs Caldwell's sloping roof. She asked for help. Elsie suggested calling the fire brigade. Brian got a ladder and climbed up. Elsie held ladder. Paul heard ice-cream van, ran out. Elsie gave him money, let go of ladder. Ladder slipped and fell. Brian on roof with cat. Cat came down alone.
Finish the story yourself.

STORY 2

ALAN, 24. **STRANGER**, 48. **POLICEMAN**. You are **ALAN**.
Alan, lives in city, looked out of flat window. Car parked outside. Stranger trying to open window. Looked respectable. Alan shouted. Stranger paid no attention. Alan rang police. Policeman arrived. Alan went down to find out what was happening, introduced himself. Stranger said it was his car, pointed to keys inside.
Finish the story yourself.

STORY 3

SALLY, 20. **JULIE**, 11. **PETER**, 10. Children's **MOTHER**. You are **SALLY**.
Sally, walking beside river with dog. Heard scream. Julie ran up, pointed to her brother, Peter, in water. Peter drowning. Sally jumped in, saved little boy. Julie ran home to get Mother. Sally looked after Peter.
Finish the story yourself.

Now tell the same story from another point of view.
In Story 1, you are Elsie. In Story 2, you are the stranger, Jack Hodges. In Story 3, you are Julie.

5.2 A day in the life

Some days are more eventful than others. In the last few days the people on this and the opposite page had a busier day than usual and something special happened that made the day memorable.

Friday, April 24th   Helen Warner, 24, actress

Last Friday began like any other day. I woke up about 10.30, had breakfast and went out to do some shopping. I cooked my lunch as usual, but didn't feel very hungry. Afterwards I sat down to read a play my agent Harry Morgan, had sent me, but I couldn't concentrate on it. Really, I was worrying all the time about my performance the night before. The audience had been very cold and I had missed two or three cues. I was wondering how long the play would last and what I would do when it came off.

Suddenly, about 3.30, the 'phone rang. It was Harry. 'Some very important people are coming to see the show tonight,' he said. 'Jake Cummings, the Broadway producer, and three or four of his advisers. So I want you to give the performance of your life.' This news depressed me even more. I spent an hour trying to make up my mind what to wear, but finally got to the theatre as usual about 6.15. Backstage, everyone was talking at the same time, arguing about what had gone wrong on Thursday night. Harry came to my dressing-room. He wanted to give me confidence, but made me feel worse.

The first act went quite well, but I was still worried. Jason Andrews, my co-star, cheered me up. 'Don't be silly, darling,' he said. 'You were marvellous in that first scene, and you know it.' The play ended. I was in the dressing-room, taking off my make-up, when Harry appeared. 'Hurry up, he said. 'Jake Cummings is outside. He wants to take you to dinner. He was tremendously impressed. I heard him talking to his friends about a contract for the autumn. Don't keep him waiting.' Of course I didn't. We had a wonderful dinner and I'm going to New York in August to start rehearsals.

● **Activity 4**

The story above is told in chronological order, but the writer emphasises the main events of the day in two ways: 1) the main events are given more space; 2) the most important moments are indicated by using conversation. Find the main events and say why they were important.

● Activity 5 — group work

Use the notes below to write similar accounts to the one opposite of a day in the life of each of the characters. Emphasise the main events by giving them more space and using dialogue where you think it is necessary.

Monday, April 27th - David Cobb, 22, reporter on evening newspaper

10.00   Arrived at office in town centre. Boss gave him two stories to cover in afternoon. Neither very interesting. Talked to friends.

11.30   Went to pub for early lunch. Saw demonstration of unemployed workers coming. Demonstrators attacked by group in black leather jackets. Police trying to separate them.

11.40   Ran back to office. Saw Doug Patton, photographer. Hurried back to scene of demonstration.

11.45   Fighting between rival groups, stones thrown. Policemen hurt.

12.00   Order restored. Interviewed leader of demonstrators. Spoke to police inspector. Six people arrested. Took names.

12.30   Returned to office. Wrote account of demonstration.

2.30   No lunch. Went to cover stories of complaints at old people's home and interviewed vicar about church fund-raising.

4.00   Returned to office. Saw first edition of paper. Front page featured story of demonstration 'by David Cobb'.

Sunday, April 26th - Barbara Armstrong, 19, secretary

8.00   Woke up. Beautiful day. Rang friend Kathy. 'Let's go to the beach.'

9.00   Drove to the beach. Not much traffic. Clouds. Kathy - 'Let's go back'! Said 'No'. Weather forecast good.

10.00   Arrived at coast. Parked car. Sun came out. Lay on beach.

11.30   Went for swim. Kathy sunbathing, dark glasses.

11.40   Saw man, woman and child in small boat. Man rowing. Child fell overboard. Mother stood up, screamed. Child shouted for help. Swam to child and kept him afloat. Man pulled them on board. Rowed back to shore.

12.15   Kathy asleep. 'Where have you been?' Told her story.

1.00   Went to lunch in cafe on beach. Met two boys. Clive and Malcolm. Boys sat at their table. Kathy told story of rescue. Barbara embarrassed. Found out that boys lived in same town as they did. Spent afternoon together. Date with Malcolm next Friday.

5.3 The story of an escape

The writer was shot down over France on his return from a night raid on Germany during the Second World War. After getting rid of his parachute and flying kit, he decided to try to make his way to neutral Spain.

When I awoke it was about six o'clock and I felt very refreshed. It was a beautiful September morning, the sun was shining and the birds were singing.

My dreams stopped abruptly when I heard the sound of snapping twigs. Someone else was in the wood only a few yards away. I did not wait to see who it was, but I could vividly imagine a German soldier in the bushes, looking for the late occupants of the burnt-out Lancaster. I squirmed along on my elbows for a hundred yards, then ran in a crouched position, keeping under cover as much as possible.

With the aid of my compass I kept in the same direction through the woods. A mile further on I came across some recently laid barbed wire entanglements and a noticeboard with large red printing on it in French and German. I could not make out what it meant and thought it probably referred to the property being private, so I crawled under the wire. I went at a jog-trot among the undergrowth until I came to where the ground was dotted with holes. I then realised what the notice was — I was running over a German artillery range! Luckily no one was firing that morning.

I was now into open country and, running along the hedges, headed in the direction of a smaller wood. Reaching this, I came upon a sheer drop of about 50 feet covered with brambles and bushes. From where I stood I could see the River Meuse twisting its way through the fields. At the foot of the cliff ran a road which made an 'S' bend, then crossed the river by a concrete bridge. I realised that to continue in a straight line I would have to cross the bridge or swim the river.

A narrow footpath zigzagged steeply downwards through the bushes. Halfway down, on rounding a bush, I crashed right into a man trying to half-carry, half-push a bicycle up the pathway. I don't know who was more surprised, he or I.

● Activity 6

Eventually, the writer made contact with the French Resistance and escaped to Spain. Make notes on how you would finish the story in two or three more paragraphs.

● Composition

1 Tell the story of any unusual incident (a fire, an accident, etc.) you have been involved in.
2 Write about an interesting day in your life.
3 Finish the story on this page, using the notes you have made.

Prescribed books: Telling the story

Checklist

Telling the story of a novel, a play or a film is different from ordinary narrative because a work of art is considered to be permanent. Consequently, we use the Present Simple tense, not the Past Simple, as the main narrative tense.

● Use of tenses

The story/play/film **takes place/begins** in 1801. The narrator **explains** that before the story **begins**, he **met** ... (Past Simple, not Past Perfect)

At the beginning of the story, the hero **has** no idea that one day he **will become** rich. (Future, not Conditional)

While these characters **have been talking** (NOT 'were talking'), the villain **has been listening** and **has decided** (NOT 'decided') to set a trap for them. (Present Perfect Continuous and Simple tenses will be needed instead of Past Continuous and Simple.)

● Alternatives to relative clauses

In the first scene of *Pygmalion*, **Liza**, (who is) **a flower-girl**, meets **an unusual man**, (whose name is) **Professor Higgins**. (It is usual to leave out the relative clauses in such sentences.)

● Useful terms

author (of books), **writer**, **novelist** (of novels) **scriptwriter** (film dialogue), **dramatist playwright** (plays), (film) **director** (films)

People in books, plays and films are called **characters**. The **main characters** are the **hero** (e.g. Hamlet), the **heroine** (e.g. Ophelia), and the **villain** (e.g. Iago). The others are **minor characters**.

Novels are divided into **chapters**, and occasionally, **books** or **parts;** plays into **acts** and **scenes**; films into **scenes** and **shots** (one particular camera picture); television serials into **episodes**.

Scenes in plays are divided into **dialogue** and **speeches** (one character speaking for a long time); actors speak **lines**.

Novels are **read** by **readers**.

Plays are **acted** on the **stage** in front of **audiences** in **theatres**.

Films are **made** in **studios** on the **set**. (specially built background using natural scenery)

A film is **shown** on the **screen** to a **cinema audience**.

Television programmes are **watched** by **viewers**.

6.1 Writing a synopsis

● Telling the story

Because a work of art is permanent, we use the Present as the main time reference in describing what happens, not the Past. The only exception (see line 4 below) is when the reference is to real historical fact.

Read the following synopsis of the first chapters of Great Expectations *by Charles Dickens.*

Pip is an orphan, who lives with his sister and her husband, Joe, near the Thames estuary. Joe is a blacksmith. The story takes place early in the nineteenth century, when convicts were often confined in prison ships on the river. One day Pip is visiting his parents' grave when a man with a terrible expression suddenly appears. He is wearing an iron on his leg and Pip realises he is an escaped convict. The man tells Pip to get him some food and a file so that he can take the iron off. He threatens to kill the boy if he does not bring the food or if he tells anyone what he has seen. The little boy goes home and steals the food from his sister's cupboard and the file from the blacksmith. The next morning, as early as he can, he goes to find the convict and gives him what he asked for. Although he is terrified, he cannot help feeling sorry for the man. But he has no idea that one day the convict will become rich and remember his kindness.

● Activity 1

The account below is presented as narrative in the past. Change the tense of the verbs in this account to describe what happens in the play.

Pygmalion (George Bernard Shaw)

One rainy night in 1912, a number of people were waiting for taxis in the entrance to a church in London. Liza, a flower-girl, was selling flowers. A stranger in the background was listening to everything that was said, and taking notes.

An old gentleman came in out of the rain and Liza tried to sell him some flowers. A man in the crowd warned her that there was a policeman nearby taking notes and that he might arrest her for begging. She got very upset, but the note-taker said she did not need to worry. He told her and some other people which part of London they came from. It turned out that he was Professor Higgins, an expert in accents, and the old gentleman was Colonel Pickering, another expert, who had come from India to meet him. Higgins told Pickering that everyone in England was judged by their accent and that he could train a girl like Liza to speak like a duchess, so she would be accepted everywhere. He gave Pickering his address and threw some money to the girl. Liza had heard the conversation and thought she might take advantage of Higgins's challenge.

When you are studying a set text, you must remember the order of events. When you have finished reading a chapter of a novel or a scene from a play, make notes on the main events as a reminder. You can make notes in short sentences, or in note form (see page 34) provided you are able to expand them into correct sentences in your compositions.

The Third Man (Graham Greene)
Note: Up to this point, Calloway, the narrator, has explained that he met Rollo Martins at Harry Lime's funeral and told us what happened to Martins before he reached the cemetery.

Note from the numbers given which parts of the original text relate to the action of the story and how they become five short sentences, fitted into a synopsis of the whole chapter.

Martins goes to the cemetery and in this way meets Calloway.
1 There are only four people at the funeral, apart from Calloway.
2 Calloway notices Martins is upset, like the girl.
3 He has been investigating Lime's past so he asks Martins to give him a lift.
4 Calloway's driver follows.
5 They go for a drink. Martins talks about his school days with Lime. Calloway says Lime was a racketeer...

THE THIRD MAN

way away with her hands over her face, and I stood twenty yards away by another grave, watching with relief the last of Lime and noticing carefully who was there — just a man in a mackintosh I was to Martins. He came up to me and said, "Could you tell me who they are burying?"

"A fellow called Lime," I said, and was astonished to see the tears start to this stranger's eyes: he didn't look like a man who wept, nor was Lime the kind of man whom I thought likely to have mourners — genuine mourners with genuine tears. There was the girl of course, but one excepts women from all such generalisations.

Martins stood there, till the end, close beside me. He said to me later that as an old friend he didn't want to intrude on these newer ones — Lime's death belonged to them, let them have it. He was under the sentimental illusion that Lime's life — twenty years of it anyway — belonged to him. As soon as the affair was over — I am not a religious man and always feel a little impatient with the fuss that surrounds death — Martins strode away on his long legs back to his taxi. He made no attempt to speak to anyone, and the tears now were really running, at any rate the few meagre drops that any of us can squeeze out at our age.

One's file, you know, is never quite complete, a case is never really closed, even after a century,

THE THIRD MAN

when all the participants are dead. So I followed Martins. I knew the other three, I wanted to know the stranger. I caught him up by his taxi and said, "I haven't any transport. Would you give me a lift into town?" "Of course," he said. I knew the driver of my jeep would spot me as we came out and follow us unobtrusively. As we drove away I noticed he never looked behind — it's nearly always the fake mourners and the fake lovers who take that last look, who wait waving on platforms, instead of clearing quickly out, not looking back. Is it perhaps that they love themselves so much and want to keep themselves in the sight of others, even of the dead?

I said, "My name's Calloway."

"Martins," he said.

"You were a friend of Lime?"

"Yes." Most people in the last week would have hesitated before they admitted quite so much.

"Been here long?"

"I only came this afternoon from England. Harry had asked me to stay with him. I hadn't heard."

"Bit of a shock?"

"Look here," he said, "I badly want a drink, but I haven't any cash — except five pounds sterling. I'd be awfully grateful if you'd stand me one."

It was my turn to say "Of course". I thought for

6.2 Using a synopsis

A synopsis can help you to write a short composition telling the story of part of a book or as part of a composition on the book as a whole, in answer to a more general question. The notes below are a synopsis of the first two chapters of a novel.

Wuthering Heights (Emily Brontë)

Chapter 1. Lockwood (narrator) rents house from Heathcliff. Goes to Wuthering Heights. Not welcome. Forbidding house on moors full of frightening dogs. Returns following afternoon. Snowstorm beginning.

Chapter 2. Met by Joseph and young woman (Cathy). Thinks she is Heathcliff's wife. She is rude — no tea. Heathcliff comes in, Lockwood given tea. Lockwood — Heathcliff's wife? Heathcliff — No, daughter-in-law. Lockwood supposes husband is young man nearby (Hareton). Young man angry. Heathcliff — 'not my son'. Lockwood wants to go home. Takes lantern. Attacked by dogs. Heathcliff laughs. Zillah (maid) puts Lockwood in bedroom, without telling Heathcliff.

Question: Describe the scene at the beginning of the novel when Lockwood first goes to Wuthering Heights.

The story begins in 1801. Mr Lockwood has rented a house in Yorkshire, so he goes to visit his new landlord, Mr Heathcliff, at his forbidding house on the moors nearby, Wuthering Heights. He is not welcomed and the house is full of frightening dogs, but he decides to return the following afternoon, although a snowstorm is beginning.

This time he is met by an old servant, Joseph, and a beautiful young woman. He thinks she is Heathcliff's wife, but she does not invite him to tea, and when Heathcliff comes in, asks his permission before pouring Lockwood a cup. When Lockwood innocently refers to her as Heathcliff's wife, he is told she is his daughter-in-law, so he supposes she is married to a rough young man who has come in and is sitting silently in the background. This makes the young man angry, and Heathcliff says he is not his son. No one resolves the mystery, so Lockwood asks for help to find the way home. Since no one will do anything for him, he takes a lantern to light his way over the moors but is attacked by the dogs. Heathcliff just laughs, but the maid Zillah, rescues him and puts him in a bedroom in the house without telling her master.

The same synopsis can be useful as part of an answer to a more general question. Notice here that: 1) only the important details are mentioned; 2) in this case, we assume that the reader is familiar with the development of the whole story, and understands how the mystery was resolved.

Question: How does Emily Brontë build up the atmosphere of mystery and horror at the beginning of *Wuthering Heights*?

From the beginning of the novel, by using an innocent visitor from the south, Mr Lockwood, as the narrator, Emily Bronte builds up an atmosphere of mystery and horror. When he first goes to the forbidding house on the moors, it is full of frightening dogs. The next day, a snowstorm is beginning, and the people are so rude and do not explain the relationships between them, so he thinks Catherine Heathcliff is Heathcliff's wife, and afterwards Hareton's wife. When we begin reading the novel, we share Lockwood's sense of mystery because we do not know why Heathcliff and Catherine seem to hate each other and why Hareton is angry when Lockwood thinks he is **Catherine's** husband.

Afterwards, Lockwood is attacked by the dogs and Zillah puts him in a bedroom, which we find out later was Catherine Earnshaw's (Catherine's mother's room.) Here Lockwood finds a diary and has a terrible dream after reading it.

● **Activity 2**

In the extract from a composition given here find: 1) details taken from the synopsis; 2) information which can only be obtained from a knowledge of the whole novel; 3) two examples of comment on the author's technique.

6.3 Plot outlines

The basic story of a novel or play can be told in very few words. You can use the same techniques in the first paragraph of a composition to establish your knowledge of the story as are used here in a cinema guide intended to give people an idea of what they would see if they went to the cinema. Notice that they tell us the main events in the story but not how it ends.

● **Composition**

1 Describe a scene from a play you have read or a film you have seen or the events in part of a novel (see Activity 1).
2 Write a synopsis of the first ten pages of a play or novel you are studying (see page 33).
3 Write plot outlines of three films you have seen recently.

ARCADIA ★★★★
Chariots of Fire: *Ben Cross, Ian Charleson. Director: Hugh Hudson.*

The story of two gold medallists at the Olympic Games in Paris in 1924. One is a student at Cambridge, not really accepted by the authorities because he is Jewish; the other, the son of a Scottish missionary. Both want to win but for very different reasons. In each case, winning means more than victory in the Games alone.

CENTRAL ★★
The Postman Always Rings Twice: *Jack Nicholson, Jessica Lange. Director: Bob Rafelson.*

During the Great Depression in the U.S.A., in 1929, a hitch-hiker arrives at a bar a long way from the main road. Attracted by the beauty of the barkeeper's wife, he agrees to work there. The two fall passionately in love, and she suggests that they should kill her husband and run the bar themselves.

METROPOLE ★★
Stagecoach: *Claire Trevor, John Wayne. Director: John Ford.*

A stagecoach escorted by soldiers is crossing the American West. The passengers form a typical cross-section of Westerners. When they reach a staging-post, the escort cannot accompany them any further. They vote to continue their journey, however, although they must pass through territory at the mercy of Geronimo and his band of Apaches.

PALACE ★
Rocky III: *Sylvester Stallone, Talia Shire. Director: Sylvester Stallone.*

Rocky Balboa has won the World Heavyweight Boxing Championship and his career is going well. Nevertheless, when a statue in his honour is unveiled in Philadelphia, he announces his retirement. He changes his mind, however, when he is challenged by a powerful rival.

SAVOY ★★★

Becket: *Richard Burton, Peter O'Toole. Director: Peter Glenville.*

King Henry II of England decides to make his friend, the Chancellor, Thomas Becket, Archbishop of Canterbury as a political manoeuvre against the Pope. But when Becket becomes Archbishop everything changes. Thomas feels morally obliged to fulfil his responsibility to God and defend the priests. The King convinces his followers that Becket must be put to death.

STUDIO ★★
Close Encounters of the Third Kind: *Richard Dreyfuss, François Truffaut. Director: Steven Spielberg.*

Several mysterious, inexplicable events take place one after another in different parts of the world. Eventually a child of four is kidnapped by beings from outer space. These beings are in contact by telepathy with their masters, who will arrive later on in spaceships and communicate with humanity by means of music.

TIVOLI ★
Nickelodeon: *Ryan O'Neal, Burt Reynolds. Director: Peter Bogdanovich.*

In 1910, a new form of entertainment is becoming popular. For only a nickel people can see moving pictures accompanied by piano music. By chance, a young lawyer meets one of the first directors, who is fighting against a powerful company that is trying to monopolise the business. The lawyer begins working in the cinema and eventually becomes a director. One day he arrives at a small Californian town called Hollywood.

VICTORIA ★★
The Guns of Navarone: *Gregory Peck, David Niven. Director: J. Lee Thompson.*

During the Second World War, the Germans are planning an attack in the Aegean Sea which will cut off the English forces there. The Allies decide to send six destroyers to rescue the garrison. But to reach their destination, the ships must risk coming under fire from the guns on the island of Navarone.

Description: Places

Checklist

● **Passive forms and usage**

In writing about places, we often need to use the Passive, because we are more interested in the building or the town, for example, than in the person who built it.

The Duke of Leaton **built** this castle in the twelfth century. (Active)
The castle **was built** in the twelfth century (by the Duke of Leaton). (Passive)

Note that the agent (**by ...**) is not always required.

Study Reference Section — Active and Passive, page 155.
See Book 3, Exercises 38A—C.

● **Prepositions of time**

In any description of this kind, the correct use of prepositions of time is also important.

Study Reference Section — Prepositions of time, page 149.
See Book 3, Exercise 9.

● **Defining and non-defining relative clauses**

The Duke **who built this castle** was known as Fulk the Brute. (**Who built this castle** tells us which Duke we are talking about.) (Defining)
This castle was built by the first Duke of Leaton, **who was known as Fulk the Brute**. (**Who was known as Fulk the Brute** is additional information about the Duke, but the first clause could be a complete sentence in itself.) (Non-defining)

Study Reference Section — Relative clauses, page 157.
See Book 3, Exercises 10A—C.

● **Where (relative adverb)**

I went back to the town **where** I was born. (Defining the town.)
I went back to Farley, **where** I was born. (Naming the town, and giving further information. Non-defining; notice the punctuation difference.)

See Book 3, Exercise 10D.

● **Past Simple, used to and would**

Shakespeare **was born**, **lived** and **died** in England. (We use the Past Simple tense, both for continuous actions — **living** — and single actions — **dying**.)
I **used to live** in Farley. (Past form only, always implying that now the action/situation is different, i.e. I live somewhere else now.)
Whenever I visited Farley, I **would call** on my old friends. (**Would** is used for repeated action in the past.)

See Book 3, Exercise 11.

7.1 Famous buildings

● **Dialogue** 🔲

A guide is showing a group of tourists round Leaton Castle.

Listen to the dialogue.

GUIDE The castle was built in the twelfth century by the first Duke of Leaton, who was popularly known as Fulk the Brute.

TOURIST In my book it says he was called Fulk de Bréauté.

GUIDE Yes, sir. Remember I said that he was *popularly* known as Fulk the Brute — and with good reason! Now, ladies and gentlemen, the tower on your right was added in the fifteenth century, after the Wars of the Roses. It is now occupied by the present Duke and his family.

TOURIST Are you sure the castle wasn't built in the thirteenth century? It says here...

GUIDE Yes, sir. I am quite sure. The tower on the right, then, has been partly restored in the present century, and the Duke hopes that the restoration work will be finished in two years' time.

TOURIST You know, my book does say the castle was built in the thirteenth century.

GUIDE Then I'm afraid your book is wrong, sir. The castle was begun in 1108 and completed in 1144. Parts of it were destroyed, of course, during Simon de Montfort's rebellion in 1264, and had to be rebuilt afterwards, at the end of the thirteenth century.

TOURIST Yes, that's what my book says!

GUIDE No, sir. Your book apparently says the castle was built in the thirteenth century, not rebuilt. There is a difference. Now let us pass to the great dining-hall of the castle. Tea will be served there at four o'clock.

TOURIST Er, just one more question. When the present restoration work has been completed, will the whole castle be open to the public?

GUIDE No, sir. As I said, the West Tower is occupied by the Duke and his family, and that part of the castle will be kept private.

TOURIST Kept private? Why? I was told we'd be shown the whole castle, and now it seems we're only going to be shown half of it.

GUIDE The West Tower is kept private, sir, and will continue to be kept private because the Duke wants somewhere to relax after a hard day's work.

TOURIST How do you know that? It doesn't say anything about that in my book.

GUIDE I know that, sir, because I am the Duke!

● Activity 1

Using the information given below, write a short guidebook description of Salisbury Cathedral and the Taj Mahal.

SALISBURY CATHEDRAL
Begun: about 1200
Main building finished: about 1284
Built of: limestone and marble
Plans prepared by: Nicholas of Ely and Elias of Dereham
Tower and spire added: 1334-1380
Architect: Richard Mason
Alterations made: 1787-1793
Restoration work begun: 1863
More restoration work begun this century: 1959

TAJ MAHAL
Built: in Agra, India, in the seventeenth century
Begun: 1632
Finished: 1654
Built for: the Emperor Shah Jahan to honour the memory of his wife, Mumtaz Mahal
Plans prepared by: the architect Ustad Isa
Number of workmen employed in construction: 20,000

7.2 Historic towns

● **Activity 2**

Note the order of the paragraphs and decide
what information is presented in each. How
many of these paragraphs give reasons for
visiting Brighton? What are the reasons?

BRIGHTON AND HOVE
(East Sussex)

Population 234,437 (including Hove)
Early closing days: Wednesday and Thursday
VISIT: Royal Pavilion, Aquarium,
          Booth Museum (bird collection),
          Preston Manor (Chinese collection),
          The Lanes
Shipping connections with the Continent:
to Dieppe (Seajet)
London 54 miles; Portsmouth 49 miles
Southampton 63 miles.

Brighton is the largest seaside resort in the south-east of England. For many people it
seems a town of contrasts, a mixture of elegant eighteenth-century architecture and
loud, modern places of amusement.

The town was at first a fishing village and did not become popular until the
eighteenth century, when doctors began to prescribe sea-bathing as a cure for illnesses.
Rich people began to visit Brighton in large numbers, and when the Prince of Wales,
later George IV, arrived and decided to build a house there, its future as a tourist
centre was assured. The Royal Pavilion, as the house was called, was decorated in the
Chinese style popular at the time, but completely rebuilt between 1815 and 1822 in its
present Indian style. The King continued to visit it until 1827, but Queen Victoria did
not like it, and it was bought by the Brighton local authority. It is open to the public
every day and there is a special exhibition there in the summer.

The other side of Brighton, the popular seaside resort, grew up in the nineteenth
century, when the piers were built. Brighton offers all kinds of entertainment, from
concerts and plays in the theatre to the popular amusement arcades on the Palace Pier
and such local attractions as the Aquarium, established over 100 years ago, a waxworks
and an electric railway running between the Aquarium and Black Rock.

The area of old houses known as The Lanes is a very attractive shopping centre,
where visitors can buy souvenirs and antiques. The houses used to be fishermen's
cottages in the early nineteenth century, but have now been converted into shops. Not
far from The Lanes is a modern shopping centre with licensed restaurants and tables
outdoors where you can enjoy a drink in good weather.

Brighton is within easy reach of London. In fact, there is a race every year for
veteran cars from London to Brighton, held in November, and there is also the London-
to-Brighton Walk. There are horse races at Brighton racecourse, a mile from the town,
about twice a month during the season, and the races, together with Brighton's other
attractions, have made a popular day out for Londoners for many years.

● Activity 3 — group work

The description of Bath below is written in a similar way to that of Brighton opposite, but the paragraphs and sentences (except for the first in each paragraph) have been printed out of order. Put the paragraphs in the best order (the first sentence of each paragraph and the description of Brighton opposite will help you). Then take each paragraph separately and rearrange the sentences into the most logical order.

BATH (Avon)

Population: 84,670.
Early closing days: Monday and Thursday
VISIT: the Georgian city, Royal Crescent,
       Circus, Assembly Rooms
       (Museum of Costume),
       Roman Baths.
London 119 miles; Bristol 13 miles,
Southampton 63 miles.

1 a) The main attraction of Bath today, however, lies in the architecture of the eighteenth century, when it became a fashionable centre for aristocratic visitors. b) Jane Austen, the famous English novelist, lived in Bath at the beginning of the nineteenth century and mentions it as a popular meeting place. c) John Wood the Elder designed the Circus, begun in 1754, and John Wood the Younger was responsible for Royal Crescent, a design facing a sloping lawn that runs down towards a park and has an excellent view of the city. d) The Pump Room is also worth a visit.

2 a) Bath is not particularly well known for sporting activities, though there are rugby matches in winter and two golf courses nearby. b) Bristol, an interesting city of over 400,000 people, is only a short drive from Bath. c) Those who are interested in football should go to Bristol, where there are two professional teams.

3 a) Bath owes its name to the fact that it grew up around the Roman baths, which were among the largest in the Roman Empire. b) There is a reconstruction of what they must have looked like in Roman days, and Bath is still a centre for treating rheumatic diseases with the mineral waters.

4 a) Jane Austen also mentions the Assembly Rooms in her novel, *Northanger Abbey*. b) One feature that makes them particularly attractive is that sections of streets have been recreated so the costumes can be seen against the background of the period. c) At that time, as their name suggests, they were a place for people to meet for dances, but they are now the home of one of the finest costume museums in the world.

7.3 Reminiscences

HOW THE OLD PLACE HAS CHANGED!

I used to live in a small town in the Midlands. My parents' house was almost the last, at the top of the hill leading out of the town towards London. I used to go for long walks with my sister to the villages nearby, and when I was eight or nine, my parents bought me a bicycle, so I could ride to Woodington, three miles away, where my friend, Frank Marlow, lived.

Frank's father had a farm. Whenever I went there, I would play in the fields with Frank, and in summer I used to help the Marlows with the harvest. Mr Marlow was a cheerful, round-faced man. He used to milk the cows himself and deliver the milk every day, driving a horse and cart. Sometimes, if I was tired and he was just starting out on his rounds, he would put my bike on the back of the cart with the crates of milk and give me a lift home.

We moved to London when I was twelve, and for one reason or another I did not go back to Farley until last year. I expected some changes, of course, after 30 years, but I was not prepared for what I saw when I got there. I approached the town by the motorway, instead of by the old London road. As I turned off at the Farley exit, I saw rows and rows of houses stretching away up a hill. The only thing that reminded me of my childhood was a pond at the foot of the hill, where a few ducks were swimming contentedly. This seemed familiar but I did not realise where I was until I joined the London road at the top of the hill and saw the town below me and my parents' old house on the right-hand side. I was so shocked for a moment that I stopped the car.

When I was a boy, I used to throw stones into the village pond at Woodington with Frank Marlow. The pond is all that is left of the village now because the village itself is under the motorway, and the rows of houses stand where Mr Marlow's farm was. No doubt the people who live in the house where I grew up drink milk every day, as I did, but I can't believe it is as fresh as the milk Mr Marlow delivered to our door, driving his horse and cart.

● Activity 4

The passage above compares the present with the past. How does the writer: 1) establish time and place in the reader's mind; 2) explain the reason for the comparison; 3) indicate his preference for the past? How many comparisons between present and past can you find in the passage?

● Composition

1 Describe a famous building in your city or country and give some details of its history.
2 Describe a town you have visited, indicating its attraction for tourists.
3 Explain what changes have taken place in a town or village you know well.

Giving advice

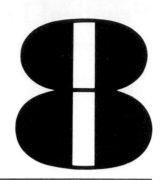

Checklist

This unit deals with advice given in different situations.

● Had better and should (ought to)

I**'d better come** with you. You may not find it by yourself. = It would be a good idea if I came with you.
You**'d better hurry!** = It would be a good idea if you hurried.
You **should take** his advice. = It would be wise to/It would be in your interest to ...
You **shouldn't smoke** so much. = It is not good for you/It is against your interest to ...

*Study Reference Section — Modals, page 149.
See Book 3, Exercises 40A—B.*

● Unless and provided

Advice also involves conditions in many cases because the advice may depend on what the conditions are. Apart from sentences using **if**, you also need to know how to use **unless** and **provided**.

Unless you follow my instructions, you will get lost. (**Unless** = if ... not, but is stronger, suggesting 'You will only avoid getting lost if you follow my instructions'.)
Provided (Providing, As long as, So long as) you take a map, you won't get lost. (These words and phrases are the real opposites of **unless**. They mean 'If, but only if, you take a map ...')

See Book 3, Exercise 41.

● Prepositions of place

In giving advice on directions, you need to understand prepositions of place thoroughly.

Come **in**!
Come **into** the shop!
The shop is **in** Oxford Street, **on** the right-hand side.
It's **on** the corner of Bond Street.

*Study Reference Section — Prepositions of place, page 147.
See Book 3, Exercise 8.*

● Have/get something done

These forms are used when people prefer others to do for them things they do not want to do or cannot do for themselves. There is little difference, except that **get** suggests more effort.

I'd like to **have** my hair **done** this afternoon. Can you arrange it?
I've got to take the car to the garage to **get** the steering **fixed**.

See Book 3, Exercise 42A.

8.1 Practical help

● **Dialogues 1-4**

Angie Taylor is a receptionist at a big hotel in central London. Tourists often come to her with their problems. Here are some of the problems she dealt with one morning last week.

Listen to these four short dialogues.

Dialogue 1

ZACK Excuse me, young lady, could you tell me where I could get the lock on my briefcase repaired? It seems to be jammed.

ANGIE Your briefcase? Well, yes, you could take it to the leather-goods shop just round the corner. I'm sure they'll do it for you.

ZACK Thanks very much. Do I turn right when I get outside?

ANGIE Yes, and then right again, and it's about two doors along.

Dialogue 2

ANNA Excuse me, I wonder if you could recommend a hairdresser's near here. My husband and I are going to a party tonight, so I want to have my hair done.

ANGIE Well, we have a very good hairdresser in the hotel, but you should have an appointment. Would you like me to see if he can fit you in today?

ANNA Yes, please. This morning, if possible.

Dialogue 3

MARIA Excuse me, but could you help me? I've got all the things I need to make some coffee in my room, but no coffee.

ANGIE That's funny. There ought to be some on the tray with the cups and the kettle. The room-maid should put a new supply in every morning when she does the room. I'll call room service and make sure you get some. It shouldn't take long.

Dialogue 4

SARA Could you help me, please? My little boy's fallen down and cut his knee. Could you tell me the way to the nearest chemist's?

ANGIE Don't worry. We've got some things here for emergencies. This cream ought to stop the bleeding, and we should have some plasters somewhere. Here's one, but it's not very big. We'd better send out for some more.

SARA No, that should be big enough. If it covers the cut, it should keep him quiet.

● **Activity 1 — pair work**

Practise dialogues where one of you is a hotel receptionist and the other a tourist who a) needs to get something repaired; b) has a problem with his/her room; c) wants advice on a good restaurant; d) asks about entertainments in the city.

● **Dialogues 5-8** 📼

Harry Moore sells newspapers outside the National Gallery in Trafalgar Square. A lot of tourists stop and ask him the way.

Listen to these four short dialogues.

Dialogue 5

JUANA Excuse me. Can you help me? Can you tell me the way to Piccadilly Circus?

HARRY Yes, of course. The easiest way is to go along this side of the square, to the right, along Pall Mall, and take the second turning on the right. That's Haymarket. Go up Haymarket, turn left at the top, and you'll see Piccadilly Circus straight in front of you.

JUANA Thanks very much.

Dialogue 6

MICHEL Excuse me. Can you tell me where the Prime Minister lives, please?

HARRY Oh, yes. Cross over the square. The main road on the opposite side is Whitehall. Go down Whitehall for about half a mile and you'll see Downing Street. You can't miss it. It's the first on the right. The Prime Minister lives at Number 10.

Dialogue 7

SILVIA I wonder if you could tell me how to get to the river. I want to cross over to get to the Festival Hall.

HARRY Yes. Cross over here at the traffic lights on the left, go along Duncannon Street and you'll see Charing Cross Station in front of you. Go down the road to the left of the station — that's Villiers Street — and you'll see some steps on the right that lead to the footbridge. You'll see the Festival Hall on the other side of the river at the end of the bridge.

Dialogue 8

KURT Excuse me. Is this the National Portrait Gallery?

HARRY No, that's just round the corner. Turn left and you'll find the entrance a little way up on the left-hand side.

KURT Thank you.

● **Activity 2**

Take it in turns to be tourists in your own town and ask the way to the main buildings, the station, etc.

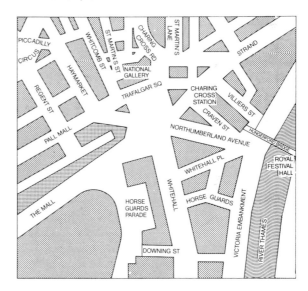

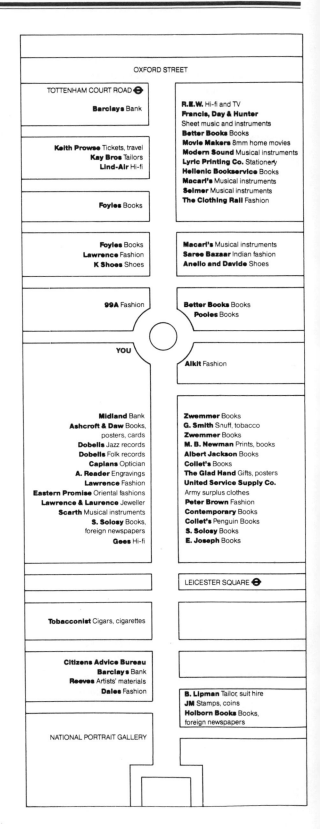

Dialogue 9

Before doing some shopping Pierre and Chantal want to change some francs into pounds. They ask a passer-by. They are standing outside Zwemmer's bookshop. (See map.)

Listen to the dialogue.

PIERRE Excuse me. I wonder if you could help us.

ANNE Well, I hope so, anyway.

PIERRE We're looking for a bank...to change some money.

ANNE A bank? Well, there's a Barclays branch just up the road, near the corner with Oxford Street.

PIERRE Do you think it's still open now? It's nearly closing time, isn't it?

ANNE Oh, so it is. Ah, but look! There's a Midland Bank branch, just across the road.

PIERRE AND CHANTAL Thanks very much.

ANNE You're welcome. You'd better hurry.

Dialogue 10

They change their money. Then Chantal decides she'd like to buy a French newspaper. They stop Sara, another passer-by.

Listen to the dialogue.

CHANTAL Excuse me. Do you think you could help us? I'm looking for a shop where I can buy a French newspaper.

SARA Well, you could try Foyles. That's just up the road on the left. Cross over Shaftesbury Avenue and carry on towards Oxford Street. You can't miss it. Or if not, walk down towards Trafalgar Square. There are quite a lot of bookshops on the way down.

CHANTAL AND PIERRE Thanks a lot.

SARA You're welcome.

● Activity 3 — pair work

Use the map of Charing Cross Road to practise asking and answering questions. Take it in turns with a partner to be a resident and a tourist. The tourist wants to buy: 1) an electric guitar; 2) some paintbrushes; 3) a packet of cigarettes; 4) a pair of dark glasses; 5) a postcard; 6) records of English folk songs; 7) some rare stamps; 8) an Indian sari; 9) some paperbacks; 10) the musical score of a Beethoven concerto. You are standing in Cambridge Circus, on the corner of Shaftesbury Avenue (see map).

● Activity 4

Where would you advise a tourist to go to buy the same things in your town?

● Activity 5

Here are nine shops and one public place in Charing Cross Road. Using the information from the street map, fill each gap in the text with the correct name: REEVES, LEICESTER SQUARE, G. SMITH'S, FOYLES, MOVIE-MAKERS, SELMER, HOLBORN BOOKS, M.B. NEWMAN, SCARTH, MACARI'S.

CHARING CROSS ROAD

Tube: Leicester Square or Tottenham Court Road.
Bus: 1 (Mon-Sat); 14, 19, 22, 24, 29, 38, 176 (Mon-Fri).

Right in the middle of the central shopping area, Charing Cross Road has none of the glamour that typifies its near neighbours Oxford Street and Leicester Square, but it attracts studious and musical people, who go there to look through books or buy musical instruments. There are dozens of bookshops, and perhaps the largest of them all is (1)........ where you can choose from over four million books.

If you've got plenty of time to spare don't forget to turn off the main street into Cecil Court, where you can find some fascinating bargains. For a few pounds you can also pick up historic postage stamps or old prints (there are some good examples at (2)........). If you want your literature right up to date, you'd better try S. Solosy shops and (3)........, where foreign newspapers are on sale.

For the musically-minded, there are several places that stock instruments, particularly guitars and amplifiers. (4)........, (5)........ and (6)........ are among them. For artists, (7)........, which stocks top-quality painting materials, is almost the last shop on the right before the road winds down into Trafalgar Square. Further up on the same side of the road, and opposite (8)........ underground station, there is a small tobacconist's shop where they sell cigars of truly prodigious lengths. And the smoker shouldn't miss (9)........ snuff shop. It is worth visiting for the rich smell alone.

It is the unusual that does well in Charing Cross Road. If you are looking for dance-band instruments, for example, you should try Scarth. If your neighbours are bored with your holiday cine films, surprise them with an all-action adventure or Laurel and Hardy comedy from (10)........

8.3 Positive advice

In my first job after university, I worked in a school in a remote mountain town in Tunisia. Before leaving England to go there, I attended a briefing course where I was told that it would be difficult for me at first to adapt to life in a Third World country, and was advised about the sort of precautions I should take to protect myself in such a strange (for me) environment.

Among other things, I was told that to avoid illness I had better boil all water before use and wash all vegetables and fruit very thoroughly; that to avoid plagues of insects I should keep my flat (and myself!) scrupulously clean; and that to avoid homesickness I should take a good collection of books and a good radio, just in case I found it difficult to make friends. Not much was said about the people, except that provided I knew French, I would not have any problems in making myself understood, as 'people speak French everywhere in Tunisia'.

All of this was sound practical advice, which I followed, and, in fact, I caught no serious illnesses, the insects left me alone, and I don't remember ever being lonely or homesick. After a month or two in the town, however, I began to be sorry that the advice had not been more positive. If you only prepare people for the worst, you may spoil their chances of enjoying the best, and if one thing is true about all foreign travel, it is this: that the more you prepare yourself for a visit and the more effort you make to understand how the people in the foreign country think and live, the more likely you are to enjoy the visit and the more you will get out of it.

Nobody told me that on the briefing course. They did not tell me, either, that unless you learn the people's own language, you will never get to know them properly; that unless you learn something about the country's history, the customs and traditions will seem meaningless; and that unless you decide to accept the foreign country for what it is without comparing it all the time with your own, you will always be an outsider who never understands what is happening around him.

● Activity 6

What sort of advice was the writer given? Put the advice into direct speech. What sort of advice would have been more useful? Put this into direct speech, e.g. **You should/You shouldn't ...**

● Composition

1 Write a letter to a friend who is coming to your country for the first time, advising him/her on the most interesting places to visit.
2 Write a letter to a friend who is very interested in shopping, indicating where he/she should go in your town for the best bargains.
3 Write a letter to a friend thinking of coming to your country, advising him/her about the weather and the kind of clothes he/she should bring at different times of the year.

Discussion: Arguing for or against

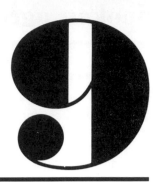

Checklist

A number of the most commonly used phrases in expressing opinions, and agreeing or disagreeing with them, are given on page 51 in the short conversations on that page.

● Conditional sentences (1)

Conditional sentences are inevitably used to a considerable extent in argument, but you should be clear about the kind of condition implied.

Boys and girls **study** better if they **are kept** apart. (General statement, using Present Simple in both clauses.)
If you **go** to boarding school, you **will** (**may**) **be** unhappy. (Specific case, using Present Simple and Future Simple or modal.)
I **would have** more sympathy with your point of view if you **made** some constructive suggestions. = You don't make constructive suggestions. (Past Simple in the **if** clause, and Conditional, **would** ... in the other.)
The only sensible argument in favour of that **would be** to say that ... (Hypothetical, without the **if** clause using Conditional, **would**...)

See Book 3, Exercise 98A.

● Must (logical conclusion and obligation)

There **must be** a logical answer to this problem. = I'm sure there is ...
You **must have been** surprised to hear Mr Smith argue that ... = I'm sure you were surprised ... (NOT 'You had to be')

Study Reference Section — Modals, page 149.
See Book 3, Exercise 43.

● Purpose clauses (1): infinitive, in order to and so as (not) to, so that

Arguments usually demand giving reasons why things happen, either using a clause with **because**, or a purpose clause.

The Government has developed the plan **to provide** employment. (The infinitive of purpose is used when there is no change in subject.)
In order to (**So as to**) **reduce** unemployment, the Government has ... (A more formal structure of the same kind.)

With double object verbs, such as **send**, the infinitive is used although the subject changes.

I sent him to the baker's **to buy** some bread.

In negative sentences, **so as not to** (**in order not to**) must always be used.

He came in quietly **so as not to** wake the baby.

When the subject changes in a purpose clause, we use **so that**.

I'm going to ask you to sit down **so that** other people can express their opinion.

See Book 3, Exercises 44A—B.

9.1 Spoken agreement/disagreement

● **Questionnaire**

If you hear someone express the opinions
given in the questionnaire below, how do you
react? Complete the questionnaire. Don't think
too long about your answers; mark your
immediate reaction.
How to answer the questionnaire:

+   That's just what I think.
+   Yes, I agree on the whole.
●   I don't know./I have no strong feelings on the matter./
    The statement is too vague for me to decide.
—   I don't think that's really true.
—   I don't agree at all. That's wrong.

	+	+	●	—	—
1 There's too much juvenile delinquency these days. It's mainly the parents' fault.					
2 Television is a menace to our society.					
3 If boys and girls are kept apart at school, they study better.					
4 Strikes should be made illegal.					
5 It's better to live in a flat than in a house.					
6 Advertising should not be allowed on radio or television.					
7 The law is too soft in its treatment of criminals.					
8 It's the Government's responsibility to provide everyone with work.					
9 Military service is a complete waste of time and money.					
10 Parents should be free to decide what sort of school their children should go to.					
11 The state should encourage couples to have large families.					
12 Animals should not be used in laboratory experiments.					
13 People should be made to use public transport and leave their cars at home.					
14 It's better to live in the country than in the city.					
15 There's more immorality than there used to be.					

● Dialogues

Listen to these short dialogues. Notice how the second speaker either agrees or disagrees with the first.

ALAN If you ask me, there's too much juvenile delinquency these days. It's the parents' fault, in my opinion.

+ BETTY I quite agree. (That's just what I think.) They should bring their children up properly.

ERIC As I see it, universities exist to do research, not to give people pieces of paper so they can get jobs as advertising agents and public relations officers.

+ FIONA On the whole, I agree with you. (In general terms, I think you're right.) But everybody can't spend his life doing research and the others need a good education, too.

IAN Don't you agree that there's more immorality than there used to be?

● JANET To be quite honest, I don't think we know enough to judge. And it depends on what you mean by immorality, anyway.

KAREN The most successful marriages result from an attraction of opposites, in my opinion.

● LESLIE You may be right. Has anyone ever done any research on it?

MAURICE In my view, boys and girls study better if they are kept apart at school.

— NELL I doubt if that's true. (I'm not sure I agree with that.) They probably have a lot of psychological problems as a result, and that's worse in the long run.

SUSAN I think the state should encourage couples to have large families.

— TREVOR On the contrary. (I don't agree at all.) Most of the world's problems are due to overpopulation. People should only have the children they really want.

● Activity 1 — pair work

Take it in turns to read the statements in the questionnaire opposite, irrespective of your own opinion. Your partner should respond appropriately, giving his/her own opinion and using the appropriate forms in the same way as the speakers above.

9.2 Written agreement/disagreement

The Carchester Herald

Cost of Parking

Sir,

I should like to draw your readers' attention to the inadequacy of the parking facilities in the centre of Carchester. The way things are organised, or rather disorganised, at present, suggests that there must be an agreement between the local authority and the police to get as much revenue as possible out of the long-suffering motorist.

Those of your readers who need to use their cars every day for business, like me, will immediately recognise that what happened to me yesterday is typical. I had to make a visit to a customer in Bridge Street to deliver some urgently needed spare parts. There is no car park within half a mile of Bridge Street so I left my car on the pavement outside the customer's shop. I avoided parking it at the kerbside so as not to hold up the traffic. When I returned, only about two minutes later, a traffic warden, who must have been hiding somewhere nearby, was already writing out a ticket and was just going to stick it on my windscreen. She refused to listen to my explanation.

If the authorities are not prepared to provide adequate parking spaces for motorists in the centre of the city, they should relax the regulations to allow people to get their work done. It is hardly surprising that there is widespread unemployment in this country if the bureaucrats are determined to make life difficult for businessmen.

R. HOGG
Overcliff Drive, Carchester

● **Activity 2 — group work**

1 People arguing a case strongly for or against something naturally use various techniques to persuade others that they are right. How does the writer of this letter to his local newspaper show, right from the beginning, that he is in sympathy with motorists and not with the police or the local authority? Find two words in the first paragraph accusing the police and the local authority.

2 He also attempts to influence readers by suggesting that he, like other motorists, is persecuted (two phrases), public-spirited (one phrase) and a hard-working, valuable citizen (four phrases). Find these phrases in the text.

3 In arguing a case, it is important: a) to explain what you are arguing about in general terms; b) to give a practical example; c) to provide an alternative solution. Do you think the writer's example justifies his case? Do you think his alternative solution is valid?

Letters to the Editor

Parking Shock

Sir,

The majority of your readers must have been surprised and shocked to read a letter from Mr R. Hogg, published in last Wednesday's *Herald*. Mr. Hogg seems to think that his own convenience and that of motorists in general are the only things that matter in our city.

I would have more sympathy with Mr Hogg if he limited himself to making constructive suggestions to improve the situation. No doubt his problems would be partly solved if the local authorities built a multi-storey car park in the city centre, instead of encouraging motorists to use public transport. All the same, judging from the tone of Mr Hogg's letter, I suspect that motorists who are so careless of pedestrians' safety that they would rather park their cars on the pavement than hold up the traffic would probably be too lazy to use a multi-storey car park if they had to walk a few hundred yards to their destination afterwards.

My main reason for writing, however, is much more important. Is Mr Hogg aware that, according to figures issued by the Department of Transport, 13,000 people were knocked down in Britain last year because of cars being illegally parked either on the pavement or on crossings? In fact, although the total pedestrian casualty rate has fallen over the last ten years, there has been an increase in accidents caused when pedestrians have to step out into the road to avoid parked cars on the pavement and cannot see oncoming traffic.

I, for one, cannot share Mr Hogg's view that the authorities are prejudiced against 'long-suffering motorists'. On the contrary, I think the penalties for dangerous parking should be made severe enough to deter all motorists from breaking the law in this way.

A. WALKER,
Proudfoot Lane, Carchester

● **Activity 3**

The letter above was written in answer to the letter on the opposite page. Study the technique used and answer the following questions.

1 How does the writer make clear to us which letter he is replying to?
2 Although Mr Walker appears to be reasonable, he tries to prejudice the reader against the first writer. Find the sentences suggesting he is reasonable, and two adjectives in the second paragraph which try to influence us against Mr Hogg.

3 The second and third paragraphs of the letter both contain an attack on motorists like Mr Hogg. Which attack is more effective, in your opinion, and why?
4 In what way is the end of Mr Walker's letter similar to Mr Hogg's, and in what way is it different?

● Activity 4 — group work

Divide into two, four or six groups. One side must write a letter to a newspaper arguing that advertising should not be allowed on radio or television.

Main argument

Radio and television are the most influential means of communication in our society and should be free from the pressures of commercial interests. Example: the U.S.A., where companies advertising products sponsor programmes.

Secondary arguments

1 Radio and television are a means of educating people but can be used to prevent them from learning.
2 The influence of advertising means poor-quality programmes because advertisers don't want people to think too much.
3 Advertising makes people buy things they don't need.
4 Programmes are always spoilt by advertisements interrupting them.

The other side must write a letter protesting against having to pay for state radio and television.

Main argument

In this country people have to pay to see programmes they don't like which could be financed by advertising. Example: Great Britain (the BBC), especially until the 1950s when commercial television was introduced (although everyone still has to pay the licence fee).

Secondary arguments

1 People have a right to choose programmes, like products.
2 Newspapers depend on advertising but the press is free.
3 If the state controls all radio and television, the Government can use it for propaganda.
4 The Government can control advertising by limiting the amount of time available.

Make notes for a letter to the editor of a newspaper, bearing in mind the following:
1 Give a reason for writing.
2 State your argument, connecting the points you want to make. In doing so, try to support your argument with practical examples from your own experience or knowledge.
3 Look at the other side's arguments and answer or try to destroy as many of them as possible.
4 Reach a logical conclusion. The four points listed should make four separate paragraphs.

● Composition

1 Write an article defending any of the statements on page 50 where you have answered + except numbers 6 and 13.
2 Write a letter attacking any of the statements on page 50 except numbers 6 and 13. Choose an example where you have replied -.

Making plans

Checklist

● **Use of tenses — Present and Future**

The use of future tenses in relation to making plans is as follows:

I**'m going to** be a pilot when I leave school. (Personal intention)
He**'s arriving** on Thursday. (Previously planned)
His flight **arrives** in Paris at 2.20. (Fixed timetable)
The President **will spend** four days in Britain. (Official statement, given to the press in a press release)

● **Future time clauses**

Other tenses may be required apart from those already listed in Unit 1. Study the following examples.

When (whenever) he **comes** to see us, he **causes** trouble. (Present Simple in both clauses to describe what happens every time he comes.)
When you**'ve booked** the tickets, please **ring** my office. (or: ...you**'d better ring** my office; or: ...**will/would** you **ring** my office, please.) (The Present Perfect tense is often used instead of the Present Simple in future time clauses to indicate completed action.)

See Book 3, Exercises 95, 96A—B.

● **In case**

In case means 'because ... may'. It does not mean 'if'.
In case is followed by the Present tense when it refers to the future, by the Past when the main verb is in the past.

We'd better look at the flight timetable **in case** there **are** any problems.
I'd better warn him **in case** he **doesn't know**. (= because he may not know)
I checked the flights **in case** there **were** problems. (= because there might have been problems)

See Book 3, Exercise 45.

● **Question tags**

Question tags are often useful in confirming information about plans. They are most commonly used when the speaker expects the other person to agree with what he/she has said.

September 3rd is a Monday, **isn't it?**
He's arriving by plane, **isn't he?**

10.1 Career plans

● **Dialogue 1**

Joan Clarke is the school careers officer at Humberford Comprehensive School. She is talking to Geoff Hudson, 16.

Listen to the dialogue.

JOAN Have you thought about what you're going to do when you leave school, Geoff?

GEOFF Yes, I've given it a lot of thought, Mrs Clarke, but I've never really had any doubts. I've always wanted to be a pilot.

JOAN I see. Are you thinking of joining the Air Force, then? Most pilots begin in the services, and, after ten years or so, go into civilian flying.

GEOFF Well, if it's the only way, I'll do it, but I've read somewhere that some of the charter airlines offer a training course. I'd rather go straight into that if I can.

JOAN Yes, there are some courses like that, though you must bear in mind that a lot of airlines are in trouble at the moment, so you may not find it easy to get in. Do you know what sort of basic qualifications you'll have to have?

GEOFF Well, obviously you have to have perfect eyesight and be physically fit, but that's no problem.

JOAN No. You've always been good at sport, haven't you? Apart from that, though, they require at least five subjects in GCE, two at 'A' level and three at 'O' level, but if you really want to be sure of being accepted you ought to have more.

GEOFF Well, I'm taking eight 'O' levels this summer, and I ought to get at least six. And I'm going to stay on next year to do some 'A' levels.

JOAN Which subjects are you going to study?

GEOFF Maths, physics and chemistry.

JOAN That should be all right. Those are the ones they ask for. After that, according to this leaflet, you'll have to do an eighteen-month training course once they've accepted you, and when you've got your pilot's licence, you can join an airline to start your operational training.

GEOFF That's fine. That's just what I want to do.

JOAN Well, you've made your mind up, and, unlike most youngsters, you know exactly what you want to do. I'm not going to try to put you off, though you realise that there's a lot of competition for interesting jobs like this these days. The main thing now is to pass your exams, and then we'll have another talk about it in a year or so's time.

GEOFF Thanks, Mrs Clarke.

● **Activity 1**

Mrs Clarke has these three 16-year-old students to advise.

TONY RICHARD
Writes poetry and stories for school paper; shy, artistic, loves language, reads a lot.

KATHY WOOD
Idealistic, sociable; good self-expression; argumentative; has travelled a lot.

TINA WYMAN
Businesslike, reads a lot, acts, in school plays; sociable, extrovert and highly persuasive.

Below are notes on the four possible careers Mrs Clarke thought of for the three, after her first interview. Which career(s) would you advise for each one?

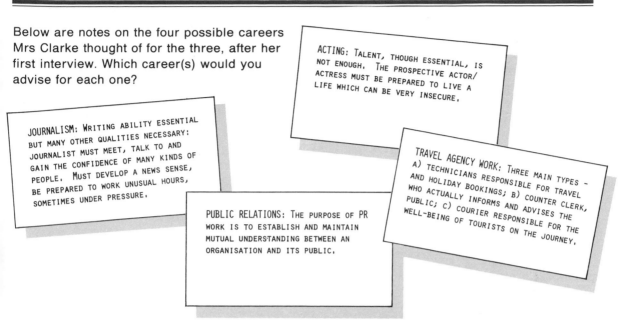

JOURNALISM: Writing ability essential but many other qualities necessary: journalist must meet, talk to and gain the confidence of many kinds of people. Must develop a news sense, be prepared to work unusual hours, sometimes under pressure.

ACTING: Talent, though essential, is not enough. The prospective actor/ actress must be prepared to live a life which can be very insecure.

PUBLIC RELATIONS: The purpose of PR work is to establish and maintain mutual understanding between an organisation and its public.

TRAVEL AGENCY WORK: Three main types – a) technicians responsible for travel and holiday bookings; b) counter clerk, who actually informs and advises the public; c) courier responsible for the well-being of tourists on the journey.

Mrs Clarke has this table of information.

CAREER	PROFESSIONAL ORGANISATION	MINIMUM ENTRY QUALIFICATION	NORMAL COURSE AND DURATION OF TRAINING
TRAVEL AGENT	Institute of Travel Agents (ITA)	Age 16+ 4'O' levels incl. English. (Maths, Geog. and 1/2 mod. langs. useful)	Student registers as member of ITA. After 5 years of part-time study and practical experience becomes associate member of ITA.
PUBLIC RELATIONS	Institute of Public Relations (IPR)	4 'O' levels	Part-time study plus appropriate practical experience leads to 1) intermediate and 2) final exam of IPR. No specific duration.
JOURNALISM	National Council for the Training of Journalists (NCTJ)	At least 3 'O's incl. Eng. Lang. and Lit. but higher standards advised. 1 'A' desirable.	Join newspaper. 6 months' probation working for paper. Then 3 years on paper, learning basic skills, plus part-time study in Further Education courses on English, shorthand, law, politics, etc.
ACTING		None specified	2/3 years of full-time study at Drama School

10.2 Travel arrangements

TELEX TEXT   27-8-1983

ATTN MALCOLM WEBSTER
MANAGING DIRECTOR
CANNIC (EUROPE)
LONDON

REFERRING YOUR TLX TL-81-405, HEREWITH SCHEDULE OF MY COMING
VISIT TO OUR REPRESENTATIVE OFFICES IN EUROPE : ARRIVAL LONDON
HEATHROW THURS 3RD SEPTEMBER, FLIGHT AC177 AT 12.15. PROPOSE
VISIT PARIS 8TH, MUNICH 9TH, MILAN 11TH, BARCELONA 12TH,
13TH, RETURN LONDON EVENING 14TH. CATCHING FLIGHT BA 622,
LONDON-MONTREAL, SEPT 15TH, DEPARTURE 11.20. KINDLY ARRANGE
INTERNAL EUROPEAN FLIGHTS AND ALL HOTEL ACCOMMODATION (SUITE).
ENSURE FULL PRESS COVERAGE OF VISIT. FOR SEPT 14TH PLEASE BOOK
HEATHROW SHERATON HOTEL. THANKS.

CARLTON C. CHASE,
PRESIDENT
CANNIC INTERNATIONAL
TORONTO.

● **Dialogue 2**

Malcolm Webster has received a telex from the president of the international company he works for, and is discussing it with his secretary, Fiona.

Listen to the dialogue.

MALCOLM I suppose you've seen this telex from the President, Fiona. As usual, they've left us to make all the arrangements, and that means you, I am afraid. I must talk to Jim Thomson about a press release.

FIONA Would you like me to book all the flights and hotels, Mr Webster?

MALCOLM The flights, yes. When you've done that, you'd better ring all the representatives and leave it to them to arrange hotels. They'll know the best places locally. When Carlton C. Chase comes to Europe, he demands perfection — in everything!

Fiona rings Claire Hamilton at Panorama Travel.

Listen to the dialogue.

CLAIRE Hello, Panorama Travel. Can I help you?

FIONA Hello, that's Claire, isn't it? This is Fiona from Cannic. Look, the big boss's coming over from Canada and we have to book a hotel for him and a lot of flights. We'd better look at the flights first in case there are any problems. Then we can book him in at the Royal Lancaster, as usual, from the 3rd to the 6th inclusive, that's four nights.

CLAIRE OK. When's he arriving?

FIONA On the 3rd, and then he's leaving for Paris on the 7th....

● **Activity 2 — pair work**

Book Mr Chase's flights. Fiona must tell Claire when he plans to visit different countries, and Claire must suggest the flights from the list given. What else must Fiona ask Claire to do, apart from booking the room at the Royal Lancaster?

Flight times:

September 7th — London-Paris, BA 362 departure 13.20 arrival 14.20

September 9th — Paris-Munich, AF 673 departure 09.10 arrival 10.30

September 10th — Munich-Milan, LH 338 departure 19.30 arrival 21.10

September 12th — Milan-Barcelona, AZ 447 departure 10.10 arrival 12.20

September 14th — Barcelona-London, IB 897 departure 13.10 arrival 14.20

Having arranged all the flights for Mr Chase, Fiona rings the Cannic Representative's secretary in Paris, Marie-France Laffitte.

Listen to the dialogue.

MARIE-FRANCE Cannic Paris.

FIONA Hello, Marie-France, this is Fiona from London. Have you had a telex from Canada about Mr Chase's visit?

MARIE-FRANCE I don't think so. When's he coming?

FIONA Well, he's coming here on Thursday the 3rd, and then he's planning to visit you on the 8th. His flight to Paris is BA 362, and it arrives in Paris at 2.20 in the afternoon on the 7th.

MARIE-FRANCE The 7th. That's a Monday, isn't it? And how long's he staying?

FIONA Till Wednesday. He leaves on the 9.10 plane for Munich. Now, Mr Webster says: Could you book him into the best hotel you can find? He wants a suite.

MARIE-FRANCE OK. That's for two nights, then, Monday and Tuesday. Have you booked his flight to Munich?

FIONA Yes, that's all settled. But you'd better warn your boss that he's coming, just in case he doesn't know!

MARIE-FRANCE Yes, of course. I'll tell him. 'Bye, Fiona.

● **Activity 3 — group work**

Make up similar dialogues between Fiona and Annemarie (in Munich), Carla (in Milan) and Teresa (in Barcelona).

10.3 Printed announcements

CANNIC

For publication from Tuesday 1st September.

Mr Carlton C. Chase, President of Cannic International, will visit Europe during the next fortnight, arriving in London on Thursday (September 3rd). Mr Chase will spend four days at Cannic's European Headquarters, accompanied by the Managing Director of Cannic's European operation, Mr Malcolm Webster. Afterwards he will fly to Paris, where he will have talks with Cannic's representative in France, M Jean-Claude Dufour, and meet the French Minister of Industry. The next country on his agenda will be West Germany, where he will visit the new Cannic offices in Munich. From Munich he will fly to Milan to inspect the Cannic distribution centre, and will then spend two days in Barcelona observing the Spanish operation.

The main purpose of Mr Chase's visit is to consider possible expansion of the European operation in view of Cannic's increasing share in the world market. A press conference will be held at the Royal Lancaster Hotel on Friday September 4th, at 7.00 p.m. Members of the press who have not received an invitation should contact Mr Jim Thomson, Press Officer, Cannic (Europe), at 01-916-2462.

Cannic Europe
8 Lisle Street
London W1

● Activity 4 — role play

(NOTE: In formal announcements referring to future plans we use the Future with **will**, but when we are talking about our plans and intentions, we use the Present Continuous and the **going to** form.)

In his Toronto office Mr Chase is talking to his secretary, Marlys, and reminding her of his plans. She asks him relevant questions. Use the press release above to make up the conversation.

e.g. CHASE As you know, Marlys, I'm visiting Europe during the next fortnight. I'm arriving in London on the 3rd.

MARLYS How long are you going to stay there, Mr Chase?

● Composition

1 Write a report on any of the young people in Activity 1. What advice would you like to give the person, and why?
2 What would you like to do when you leave school? What sort of training will you need? (If you have already left school, describe your experience in getting your first job.)
3 Write a press release describing the forthcoming visit of an important person to your country.

Narrative: Using direct and indirect speech

Checklist

Most narratives contain indirect speech in one form or another, and may also include conversations in direct speech. Examples of the main changes required in reported speech are given here.

Study Reference Section — Direct and reported speech, page 157.
See Book 3, Exercises 46A—C, 47A—B.

● **Statements**

Here you must mainly observe the changes in tense.

'**I'm going** the same way as you are.' — She said she **was going** the same way as I was.
'I **work** in London.' — He said he **worked** in London.
'I'**ll show** you the way to the house.' — She said she **would show** me the way to the house.
'I'**ve seen** that film before.' — He said he **had seen** the (that) film before.
'I **lived** in Italy when I **was** young.' — She said she **had lived** in Italy when she **was** young. (Note that we do not usually change **was** or **were** when **had** has already appeared in the sentence.)
'You **can** see the house from **here**.' — She said we **could** see the house from **there**. (**May** changes to **might**.)

● **Imperative forms for command and request**

Here you must remember the use of **ask** and **tell** with the infinitive.

'**Please help** me.' — She **asked me to help** her.
'**Don't shout**.' — I **told him not to shout**.

● **Questions**

Here, apart from the changes in tense, pay special attention to word order — subject before verb form.

Questions without a question word require **if** or **whether** in indirect speech; question words are repeated.

'**Are you** tired?' — She asked me **if I was** tired.
'Where **does she live**?' — He asked me **where she lived**.

Note that in real life, tense changes do not always involve changes to time reference, or from **this** to **that**, or **here** to **there**.

'What did you ask Maria?'
— 'I asked her **where she lives**.' (We use **lives**, not **lived** because she still lives there.)

But in narrative these changes will always be required.

I asked Maria **where she lived**.

11.1 Reporting conversations

● **Dialogue 1**

It is Sunday morning. Ian Garrett has just arrived in a small town by train. He is waiting for a taxi outside the station. Jill Mullins, 15, comes past with her Alsatian dog, Pat.

Listen to the dialogue.

IAN Excuse me, can you tell me where Vine Cottage is?

JILL Oh, yes. It's not far. It's about a mile away, along the main road. You can't miss it.

IAN I see. I really need a taxi. This case is rather heavy.

JILL I don't think you'll get one on Sunday morning.

IAN Oh, well. I suppose I'd better walk, then.

JILL I'm going that way myself. I'll show you the way. Are you going to see the Bassetts?

IAN The Bassetts?

JILL Yes, they live at Vine Cottage, but I haven't seen them for a month or so. The postman said they'd moved to the coast. I thought it might save you a wasted journey.

IAN Ah, yes. Well, I've rented the cottage for the summer. I don't know the owner's name. I did it through an estate agent.

JILL It's funny, but I'm sure I've seen you somewhere. You're not an actor, are you? Do you ever appear on TV?

IAN No, I'm not an actor. As a matter of fact...

JILL I know now. Your picture was in the paper yesterday. I'm sure it was you. My God! Pat!

IAN What's the matter?

JILL Now, don't try to do anything silly. Pat's a trained guard dog and he'll have you if I give the word. You're one of the men the police want to see about the bank robbery in London. Pat!

IAN You're making a mistake. You can ring the police and ask them, if you like.

JILL I'm sure it was you. I never forget a face.

IAN I've just had an idea. You don't read crime stories, do you?

JILL No. My Dad does, though. Good lord! I'm very sorry. I've just realised what happened. I was reading the paper yesterday, and Dad was sitting opposite me with his crime story, and your face was on the back cover. Oh, dear!

IAN Just as well you remembered. I've come down here for some peace and quiet to write another book, in fact. Would you tell Pat you've solved the mystery? I need both hands to type with, and I'd rather not get bitten.

● Reported dialogue 1

When Jill got home she told her father what had happened.

JILL It was very embarrassing. I saw this man standing outside the station and he asked me where Vine Cottage was. I said I'd show him the way. I wondered if he was going to see the Bassetts. Jack, the postman, said they'd moved to the coast, and I thought it might save him a wasted journey. But the embarrassing thing was what happened next. I suddenly thought I'd seen him somewhere. I couldn't think where it was, and then I remembered seeing his picture in the paper yesterday. I shouted to Pat and warned the man not to do anything silly or the dog would bite him. You see, I was sure he was one of the men the police want to see about that bank robbery in London. Of course, he said I was making a mistake. I was a bit doubtful, and then he asked me if I read crime stories. I suddenly realised what had happened. I was reading the paper yesterday, you were sitting opposite me with your crime story, and his face was on the back cover. His name is Ian Garrett.

DAD Really? I'd like to meet him. He must be an interesting fellow. He writes very well.

JILL Well, you will, because, of course, I apologised and I've asked him to tea. Actually, he's come down to write another book. Perhaps he'll tell you all about it.

● Activity 1

1 When we relate conversations to other people, we do not usually repeat everything that was said as a dramatic dialogue, but use indirect (reported) speech. Even then, of course, we do not report everything but only the important details. Find a) all the details that are directly reported from the conversation, and notice the changes in tense; b) statements that summarise parts of the conversation; c) additional remarks that comment on the story and help explain it.
2 Why do you think that Jill says 'yesterday', and not 'the day before' or 'the previous day', when she is telling the story?
3 Ian Garrett writes to a friend, telling him about his experience. Tell the story again from his point of view. Remember that some details may seem more important to him than to Jill (e.g. his case was heavy, he was afraid of what would happen if the dog bit him).

11.2 Summarising conversations

● **Dialogue 2** 📼

Jenny, Jane and Tom are in the lift, going back to their office on the fifth floor after lunch. There is another man in the lift.

Listen to the dialogue.

JANE OK. Everyone for the fifth floor? (*She presses the button.*)

MAN Oh, actually, I want the third. (*He presses the emergency stop and then the third floor button.*) What's the matter with it? Now it won't start.

JENNY No. it looks as if we're stuck between floors.

MAN Good heavens! I can't stand being in a confined space! I suffer from claustrophobia.

TOM It's a pity you didn't think of that when you pressed the stop button. (*The man starts hitting the door.*) Now don't panic! I doubt if anyone can hear us. The walls are pretty thick.

JENNY Isn't there an alarm you can press?

JANE Yes, here it is. (*She presses the alarm.*) Someone will hear that, I imagine.

MAN Oh, God! How long do you think we'll be stuck here?

TOM I've no idea. Luckily, we're not very far up. If the cable broke, we wouldn't be killed.

JANE That's very comforting! Thanks for cheering us up.

JENNY I can't help laughing, really. Mr Connors is waiting to dictate some letters when I get back. He'll never believe me when I tell him I've been here all the time.

(*A few minutes later.*)

MAN I can't stand this any longer. I'm going to break the door down.

JANE Don't be silly! They know we're here. Just be patient.

TOM Well, I'll tell you another joke to pass the time.

(*The lift starts moving.*)

JENNY Thank heavens for that! I don't think I could have stood another one of your stories.

● Reported dialogue 2

When she met her boyfriend, Roger, the same evening, Jenny told him what had happened.

JENNY You'll never guess what happened to me at lunchtime today. I was stuck in the lift for half an hour.

ROGER Really? How did that happen?

JENNY Well, some impatient man pressed the stop button because he wanted to get out at the third floor, and we had passed it. Then the lift wouldn't start again. It was quite funny, really, because Mr Connors was waiting to dictate some letters to me, and I knew he wouldn't believe me when I told him where I had been. But the man panicked. 'I can't stand being in a confined space!' he shouted. Then he said he was going to break the door down. Fortunately, Jane and Tom Crane were with me. They told the man to keep calm, and Tom kept telling awful jokes to pass the time. In the end the lift started again. Mr Connors was furious when I got back to the office, but of course Jane said it wasn't our fault.

● Activity 2 — group work

Notice that: a) Jenny first arouses Roger's interest in the story. How does she do this? b) In telling it, she does not usually report the conversation but only the events. The exceptions are when the conversation is relevant to the events or creates atmosphere. Find examples of both. c) On one occasion, Jenny repeats what the man said in direct speech. This draws attention to it and gives the story dramatic effect.

Read one of the following stories and write what you think was actually said in dialogue form. Pass your dialogue to another group. Now read their dialogue and tell the story, as if you were telling a friend, using Jenny's story as a model.

1 You were talking to a friend on a street corner in an old part of town. Two cars approached slowly at right angles and bumped into each other because neither driver would give way. The drivers blamed each other angrily. When you intervened to make peace, they both shouted at you.

2 While you and your wife were shopping the baby's pram was stolen from outside the shop. A few days later you both recognised it, standing outside another house a mile away. While you were talking, a big man came out of the house with a baby and put it in the pram.

3 You were driving with a friend across a bridge when the police stopped you. You thought you had done something wrong, but, in fact, yours was the one-millionth car to cross the bridge, and the town wanted to give you a prize.

11.3 Dramatising narrative

● No Welcome at the Hotel

I once had to go to a town in the north of England on business. No one in the firm had ever stayed there before, so I asked my secretary to look through the list of hotels in the Railway Guide and try to find one for me. The two that were recommended were both full so she took a chance and booked me in at the third.

I reached the hotel at 7.30 in the evening, and the manageress, a stern old lady of about 60, showed me to my room. When I asked her what time dinner was she said there was only one sitting at 6.30, and I had missed it.

'Never mind,' I said. 'I'm not very hungry. I'll just have a drink in the bar and a sandwich.'

'Bar!' she said, raising her eyebrows. 'This is a respectable hotel, young man. If you want alcohol, you must go somewhere else.' She spoke as if a glass of beer was a dangerous drug.

I went to a pub and had some beer and sandwiches and then went to the cinema. It was half-past eleven when I returned to the hotel. Everything was in darkness. I banged on the door but nothing happened. The only sound was the church clock opposite, which suddenly struck the half-hour with such force that it made me jump. Eventually a window opened upstairs. The old lady looked out and asked me what was going on. I explained who I was and she let me in after ten minutes' wait. She was in her nightdress and her hair was in curlers. She told me severely that guests were expected to be back in the hotel by eleven o'clock.

I went to bed but could not sleep. Every quarter of an hour the church clock struck and at midnight the whole hotel shook with the noise. Just before dawn, I finally dozed off.

When I arrived at breakfast, everyone else had nearly finished and there was not enough coffee to go round.

'Did you sleep well, young man?' the old lady asked.

'To tell you the truth, I don't think I could go through another night in that room,' I replied. 'I hardly slept at all.'

'That's because you were up all night drinking alcohol!' she said disapprovingly, putting an end to the conversation.

● Activity 3

This story contains examples of both direct and indirect speech. Underline all the examples of:
a) direct speech and change them to indirect speech;
b) indirect speech and change them to direct speech.

● Composition

1 Describe what happened on any occasion when you mistook a person for someone else.
2 Describe any event in your life which was an extraordinary coincidence.
3 Write one of the stories from Activity 2 from the point of view of any of the participants.

Prescribed books: Plot and theme

Checklist

● **Use and omission of the definite article**

Writing about the theme of a book, play or film usually demands some comment in abstract terms.

We do *not* use **the** for abstract concepts or subjects of study, even if they are preceded by an adjective or noun used like an adjective.

The main theme of *Hamlet* is revenge.
I am studying **literature**. (chemistry, mathematics, Chinese)
I am studying **English literature**.
I am studying **modern English literature**.
I am studying **sixteenth-century English literature**.
Sophocles lived in **Greece**. (ancient Greece, fifth-century Athens) (Again, no definite article.)

The is used when the noun is followed by a phrase containing **of** or a relative clause. The use of **the** with 'ancient world' is because 'the world' is considered to be a unique concept.

I am studying **the** literature of England.
I am studying **the** literature (**that** was) written in England in the sixteenth century.
The Athens **of** Sophocles' time, **the** Athens **that** produced so many great works of art, was **the** centre **of** culture in **the** ancient world.

Study Reference Section — Definite Article, page 143.
See Book 3, Exercise 15.

● **Relative clauses using prepositions**

Commenting on books often requires more complex sentences involving relative clauses than other forms of writing.

Study Reference Section — Relative clauses, page 157.

Note in particular:

The society **they lived in** was one **in which** revenge was considered natural. (The contact clause, **they lived in**, can only be used if the preposition follows the verb immediately.)

12.1 Identifying plot and theme

● **Plot and theme: *Hamlet***

All stories have a plot. Ever since the first story-tellers sat down in the market place or beside a camp-fire people have been interested in what happened and, above all, in what happened next. The good story-teller keeps them guessing and organises a series of incidents that lead up to a climax. These incidents, what happens, are the plot. It is not always so easy, however, to discover what the theme of a book or a play is unless the author states it in the title — *War and Peace*, *Crime and Punishment*, *Pride and Prejudice* — and some stories, especially those of adventure, may have no real theme at all.

Hamlet is a good example of the difficulties. Most people know it is the story of a prince whose father's ghost appears and tells him that his uncle, who has since married his mother and become king, murdered him. When Hamlet has proved the ghost's story to be true, he eventually revenges the murder. Yet critics still disagree about the theme or themes of *Hamlet*. Laurence Olivier's film began by stating: 'This is the story of a man who could not make up his mind', in which case the main theme is doubt or hesitation. It seems rather an unusual theme for a play in which the hero kills three characters and arranges the death of two more! Other critics have concentrated on Hamlet's famous speech, 'To be or not to be', in which he thinks about suicide, and have suggested that the main theme is the suffering of a sensitive man obliged by circumstances to act against his will and almost incapable of doing so. For a Freudian psychologist, the theme is Hamlet's love for his mother; he really hated his father and is suffering from an Oedipus complex.

For Shakespeare's original audience the theme was revenge. The society they lived in was one in which the government was trying to persuade people to settle their family quarrels by law, instead of by duels or a vendetta. What concerned them were the circumstances in which a man was justified in taking the law into his own hands, which is also the theme of many modern films. As for Hamlet's character, Shakespeare seems to have read a recently published medical book describing the character traits of the melancholy man, most of which can be seen in Hamlet. One of them is that such men are slow to act but act rapidly and decisively once they have made up their minds.

If the theme of *Hamlet* is revenge — and Hamlet's hesitation at first is typical of one type of melancholy man — why doesn't he act immediately when he knows the truth? Of course he does, but by mistake he kills Polonius instead of the king. Afterwards, Shakespeare takes care not to give him another opportunity until the end. What some critics seem to overlook is that Shakespeare understood the importance of plot as well as theme and that he was an actor who knew from experience what audiences expect and how they react.

When Hamlet finally kills the king, he does so in the great climactic scene of the duel with Laertes, whose sword has a poisoned tip and who confesses that the king has in this way killed them both. So Hamlet dies, provoked into revenge by the king's treachery, with all our sympathies on his side. His revenge becomes natural justice. From this point of view, he is not a hypersensitive dreamer but a hero who could serve as a model for the heroes of modern Westerns.

● **Activity 1**

Decide which sections of this article refer to plot and which to theme.

● Activity 2

On the left-hand side below are plot outlines of some of the world's greatest plays and novels. Read them and decide what the themes of these plays and novels are by finding the corresponding description in the right-hand column, where the lists of themes are given out of order. See how many of the plot outlines you recognised and whether you agree with the list of themes referring to them. (Answers on page 163.)

1 A man who has been chosen as king because of his intelligence learns against his will that he has fulfilled a prophecy. He has killed his father and married his mother.

2 An old man has read so many romances that he leaves home in search of knightly adventures. He makes ridiculous mistakes but they reflect his essential nobility.

3 A boy helps a negro slave to escape, though he has been brought up to believe this is a crime. He eventually realises that the world's values are upside-down.

4 A great general trusts one of his officers, who really hates him and tells him his young wife is unfaithful. As he is middle-aged and black, he believes the lie and kills her.

5 The devil visits a clever doctor and promises him everything he can desire in life in exchange for his soul. In the end, the promise must be kept.

6 A young wife broke the law to save her husband's life. When he finds out, he blames her for it. She realises her marriage is meaningless and leaves him to find a life of her own.

A The position of women in society, bourgeois values, hypocrisy, marital relationships, finding one's true personality.

B Envy, jealousy, the destruction of love, middle-aged insecurity, colour prejudice.

C Fate, refusal to recognise the truth, intelligence, humility, physical and intellectual blindness.

D Honesty, hypocrisy, colour prejudice, the nature of real goodness, generosity, simplicity.

E Idealism, chivalry, the code of honour, truth and illusion, the nature of real nobility.

F Ambition, rivalry with God, the wish to be a superman.

12.2 Writing on a theme

● *Heart of Darkness*

Biographical data

Joseph Conrad (born Konrad Korzeniowski in Russian-occupied Poland in 1857) became a captain in the British merchant navy. *Heart of Darkness* (1902) is based on his experiences as captain of a steamer on the Congo River in what was then the Belgian Congo (now Zaire).

Plot outline based on synopsis

Captain Marlow (who stands for Conrad) tells the story to some friends of his on the Thames. He reminds them that when the first Romans came to Britain they must have regarded the natives as savages.

Marlow is engaged to captain a steamer which has broken down on the Congo River. His first impression of the Congo is of a grove where black men in the company's service are slowly dying. He hears about Mr Kurtz, the company's most successful agent up the river. The greedy men at the headquarters admire Kurtz, partly because he sends them so much ivory but also because he is a civilised man, with the best European values.

Marlow gets the steamer repaired and goes upriver with a group of Europeans to Kurtz's station. They are threatened by hostile natives but eventually reach it. (Marlow says that since then he has read Kurtz's report, which began with magnificent plans but ended with the words: 'Exterminate all the brutes.') Kurtz's house is surrounded by skulls on poles, those of natives he must have killed as a kind of savage high priest. Kurtz does not want to leave, but they take him aboard the boat, and escape down the river, pursued by the natives. Kurtz is dying. His last words are: 'The horror! The horror!' Marlow takes his letters to his fiancée in Europe. He cannot tell her the truth and says: 'The last word he pronounced was ... your name.' She keeps the illusion that Kurtz was a wonderful man.

Themes

Colonialism, civilisation and savagery, the temptations of power.

Quotations

'The conquest of the earth, which mostly means the taking it away from those who have a different complexion or slightly flatter noses than ourselves, is not a pretty thing when you look into it.'

'You should have heard him say, "My ivory". Oh, yes, I heard him. "... My Intended, my ivory, my station, my river, my ..." everything.'

'The wilderness had found him out early, and had taken on him a terrible vengeance for the fantastic invasion. I think it had whispered to him things about himself which he did not know...'

'He was hollow at the core.'

In answering a question on the theme of a book, you must show your knowledge of the story without telling the story directly. If you have noted down some useful quotations, try to remember and quote key phrases and not the whole quotation, which you may not remember.

Before reading the model composition below, look back to the information given on the opposite page and: 1) make notes of the biographical details that are relevant to the question; 2) do the same thing with the synopsis; 3) decide which of the quotations can be used and which key phrases can be picked out of them.

● **Activity 3**

Find the source on the opposite page for everything that is said in the model composition. If anything is left in the composition without a source, it is interpretation; anything left in the source material which does not appear in the composition has been left out because it is irrelevant to the question.

Question: In what ways is *Heart of Darkness* an attack on colonialism?

Conrad used his own experience as the captain of a steamer on the Congo in writing <u>Heart of Darkness</u>. From the beginning of the story, the narrator, Marlow, who stands for Conrad himself, makes us see that the Romans looked at the Britons in the same way as modern Europeans regard the natives in Africa. There is not so much difference between civilisation and savagery as people imagine.

The first impression Marlow has in Africa, of the black men dying in the grove, prepares us for the horror of the journey up the river and Kurtz's camp. Kurtz started with good intentions, believing in his civilised superiority, but ended by exterminating the natives and becoming a kind of savage god to the tribe. He did not understand the strength of the jungle and his own weakness. When he dies with the words 'The horror! The horrror!' he is referring to his own life and the way in which absolute power can corrupt a man who is apparently civilised and can make him more brutal than the brutes he says he wants to exterminate.

Marlow cannot tell Kurtz's fiancée, who stands for happily ignorant Europeans, what the Congo was really like. But he tells us that colonialism is evil, because instead of being heroic, it just means taking things away 'from those who have a different complexion'. The worst thing about it is the effect it has on the colonisers. By giving power to men like Kurtz, it can corrupt them and appeal to all the secret vices in their nature that they were not aware of until they went into the jungle. Conrad suggests that this will happen to most men, because even an exceptional man like Kurtz is 'hollow at the core'.

12.3 Literary devices

Symbol, Allegory and Personification

Films are the ideal art form for the use of symbols. An object seen on the screen, where the director can deliberately focus our attention on it, is easier to remember than in a book. A whole film can even be devoted to finding the meaning of a symbol. In Orson Welles's *Citizen Kane* a journalist tries to discover the meaning of 'rosebud', the last word the millionaire Kane spoke before he died. He never finds out, but in the last shot of the film we are shown a child's sledge being burnt, with the name 'Rosebud' painted on it. We remember that in the first flashback of the film, when Kane as a small boy was taken away from his poor parents to be educated by his rich relations, he was playing with a sledge in the snow. Rosebud symbolises the lost innocence of his childhood, the simple life he could have led.

If films often make symbols clearer, such classical literary devices as allegory and personification become more difficult. Ingmar Bergman attempted both in *The Seventh Seal*. The film takes place in the fourteenth century, when the Black Death was raging in Sweden. In the first scene, a knight who has returned from the Crusades is lying on the beach beside a chessboard. A dark figure approaches him, saying he is Death. The knight, to avoid going with him, challenges him to a game of chess, which continues throughout the film. Apart from the obvious personification of Death, all the main characters represent different attitudes to faith. The knight personifies agnostic humanism—he is a noble, kind man who cannot believe in God; the squire personifies materialism; the simple clown and his wife and child, the only ones who escape Death in the end, stand for the Holy Family; the couple are called Joseph and Mary.

The film is an allegory of humanity facing worldwide disaster; it uses real characters to describe abstract ideas and values. Yet though it is a magnificent film, the realism of the photography makes it difficult to accept the story in allegorical terms. When the knight knows that he has lost the chess game, the symbol of man's inevitable losing battle with death, he knocks the pieces over; he cannot save himself but he distracts Death's attention from the clown and his family, allowing them to escape. In human terms, the action is clear and admirable. But in allegorical terms, how can the good man who does not believe in God save the innocent, whose simple belief, according to Christian doctrine, is what saves them in any case?

Just as artists must be careful in their use of symbols, allegory and personification, we must be careful in our use of the terms. A symbol is an object that stands for something else. Allegory is the use of characters in a story that has another significance—like George Orwell's use of the animals in *Animal Farm* to describe the Russian Revolution. Personification is the use of real characters who stand for abstract conceptions. It is significant that publicists who want women to find an actress attractive say she is the personification of charm, or beauty, or vitality. When they want men to think of her as an object of desire, they call her a sex symbol.

● **Composition**

1 Discuss the main theme of the set text you are reading, showing how it is illustrated in the plot.
2 Consider the use of symbols in any film you have seen recently.

Description: Giving instructions

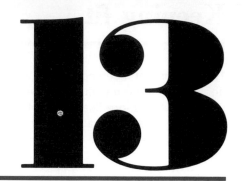

Checklist

● Imperative and alternative forms

Instructions can be given in the imperative.

Heat the mixture gently for half an hour.
Do not allow the gas to go out.

When they are a matter of advice, rather than an order, **should** is preferred.

You **should get** as much exercise as you can. You **should not attempt** difficult exercises without taking the advice of a teacher.

In specific cases, they may involve the use of a conditional or time clause, but note the use of the Present Simple.

If (When) you **want** to record a programme from the television on the video, **(you must) plug in** the connection to ....

● Gerund and infinitive in general statements

A gerund stands for a noun.

Working hard can be its own reward. (= Hard work)

It is the correct verb form to use after a preposition.

He worked all morning without **stopping**. (= without a pause)

We prefer the gerund to the infinitive at the beginning of a sentence; if we use the infinitive we normally begin the sentence with an impersonal subject, **it**.

Remembering grammatical rules is sometimes difficult.
It is sometimes difficult **to remember** grammatical rules.

Writing well is always a pleasure.
It is always a pleasure **to write** well.

See Book 3, Exercise 48.

● Clauses of concession (1): **although, even though, while**

Although and **even though** are alternatives to **but**, and preferable in descriptive prose. Because the main clause usually comes second, it has more strength than **but**, and is more persuasive for this reason.

Although (Even though) dieting is often desirable, it is unwise to attempt it without a doctor's advice. (= Dieting is often desirable, **but** it is unwise to attempt it ...)

While is used to provide a balance between the two halves of such sentences, giving them equal importance.

While the exercises we recommend are useful, there are others that will achieve the same object in about the same time.

13.1 Keeping fit

The purpose of 'keeping fit' is to avoid ill health, resist the mental and physical fatigue that makes us more likely to contract infections, and above all to feel more pleasure in being alive. Research has shown the value of a balanced diet, fresh air, sunshine, adequate rest and some form of regular exercise for everyone. If everyone followed this plan, the number of people visiting the doctor and going to hospital would be considerably reduced.

Unfortunately, although most people acknowledge the importance of physical fitness, not enough of us put this into practice; we spend too much time watching others from the comfort of an armchair or a seat in the stand at a sports stadium.

One reason why people who are physically fit live longer is that they do not put the heart under excessive strain and so they reduce the risk of heart and blood-vessel diseases. They also avoid suffering the consequences of weakened muscles, which are the cause of a great deal of back and abdominal trouble.

About 640 muscles account for about 45% of our body's weight; they must have the ability to store energy and be continually supplied with fuel by the blood. Sensible exercise, suited to each individual and preferably undertaken on the advice of a doctor, is the best insurance for meeting these requirements.

Most people have learned basic exercises at school — stretching, running on the spot, lifting weights and so on. While these are useful, some new keep-fit techniques are very popular and effective and much easier to employ. One is isometrics, a form of exercise without movement in which one muscle group is exerted against another tensed or contracted muscle group for about five to eight seconds. This form of exercise is suitable for both men and women, can be safely carried out without supervision and has the advantage that it can be performed almost anywhere — even sitting at a desk.

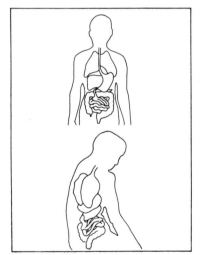

Although we have been standing upright for hundreds of thousands of years, we still show the strain by our tendency to slump forwards, curve our back, round our shoulders and shrink our chest into our abdomen. This may give us neck and back pains and make breathing more difficult. On the other hand, if our posture is too rigid, it can strain the spine.

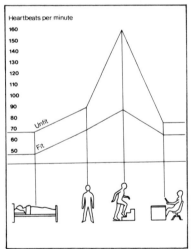

When a person is not physically fit, his heart is given an extra workload, shown by the number of heartbeats per minute required for everyday activities.

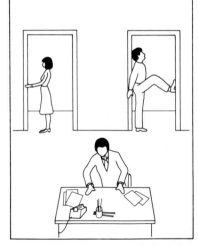

Isometric exercises. The door jamb strengthens leg and stomach muscles. Pressing the palms of the hands down with force on the desk or table strengthens the upper arms.

Yoga exercises have become increasingly popular in recent years. They emphasise harmonious co-ordination of movement, stretching and correct breathing. A few of these exercises, practised for 10-15 minutes every day, improve the whole physical system. They should nevertheless be learned under the supervision of a teacher and should never be attempted too quickly; otherwise, unused muscles will not be adequately prepared.

The Cobra

The Cat

The Half Locust

The Half Plough

The pose of the Camel

The Half Shoulder Stand

The Cobra increases the flexibility of the spine. The Cat helps the throat and chin-line and stretches the back and stomach muscles.

The Half Locust makes thighs and buttocks firmer, while the Half Plough flattens stomach muscles. The pose of the Camel makes the spine flexible, strengthens the neck and makes the jaw line firmer. The Half Shoulder Stand improves the circulation of the blood.

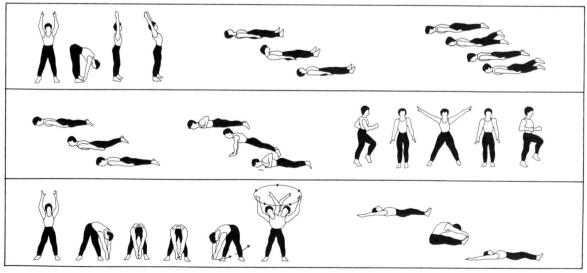

● **Activity 1 — group work**

The chart above shows some exercises which are designed to increase fitness gradually. Take it in turns to explain to others in the group how to do them.

HUNGARIAN GOULASH

This internationally famous stew is usually made from beef, though pork, veal and chicken may also be used. Different regions of Hungary have their own favourite goulash recipes. Some use fresh tomatoes, others caraway seeds, garlic or marjoram. But whatever else goes into a goulash, it always contains paprika.

PREPARATION TIME 35 minutes   COOKING TIME About 2 hours

INGREDIENTS (for 4)

1¼ pints (850 ml) stock	1¼ pounds (560 g) steak	2 level teaspoons caster sugar
Salt	1 pound (450 g) onions	3 level dessertspoons plain flour
2¼ ounces (65 g) tomato purée	2 ounces (56 g) lard	2½ fluid ounces (70 ml) soured cream
	3-4 level teaspoons paprika	

METHOD

Wipe the meat and cut off any fat and gristle. Cut it into 1½ inch (4 cm) cubes. Peel and thinly slice the onions. Melt the lard in a deep, heavy-based pan and fry the meat and onions over moderate heat until the onions are golden and the meat is sealed. Pour over the hot stock, season with salt and bring to simmering point. Meanwhile, blend the tomato purée, paprika, sugar and flour in a small bowl until smooth. Stir in a few tablespoons of the hot stew liquid.

Take the pan with the onions and meat off the heat, stir in the tomato purée mixture, blending thoroughly. Return to the heat and bring back to a simmer. Cover and leave the stew to cook over a gentle heat for about 2 hours or until the meat is quite tender. Stir occasionally.

Just before serving, stir in the soured cream and adjust the seasoning. Ribbon noodles are traditional with goulash, but boiled floury potatoes can be served instead.

● Activity 2

Complete the recipe below by referring to the numbered drawings. Each drawing corresponds to the space of the same number and shows what you should do at that stage. Fill in the missing instructions.

HOW TO COOK MOUSSAKA

The aubergine — or eggplant — is a staple vegetable of the Middle East. It is the basic ingredient in moussaka, meaning aubergine casserole; the dish may include minced beef or lamb.

PREPARATION TIME 45 minutes
COOKING TIME 35-40 minutes
INGREDIENTS (for 4)

4 aubergines	Salt and black pepper
1 large onion	1 ounce (25 g) unsalted
4-6 tablespoons olive oil	butter
1 pound (450 g) lean minced beef	1 ounce (25 g) plain flour
	½ pint (275 ml) milk
1 level teaspoon salt	1 egg
2 rounded teaspoons tomato purée	

METHOD

(1) .... Heat 1 tablespoon of the oil in a heavy-based pan and gently fry the onions for about 5 minutes, covering the pan with a lid. Add the minced beef and fry until brown and thoroughly sealed. Stir in the salt, tomato purée and stock. Season to taste with freshly ground pepper. Bring this mixture to the boil, (2) .... and simmer gently for 30 minutes or until the meat is tender and the liquid is almost absorbed. Meanwhile, peel and (3) .... Arrange them in a layer on a plate and sprinkle generously with salt; let the aubergines stand for 30 minutes to draw out the bitter juices. Drain, rinse in cold water and dry thoroughly on absorbent kitchen paper. Fry the aubergine slices in the remaining oil until golden, then drain on absorbent paper. (4) .... in the bottom of a large buttered fireproof dish or casserole. Cover with a layer of the meat, another layer of aubergines and so on, until all is used up; finish with a layer of aubergines. (5) .... over a low heat and stir in the flour. Cook gently for 1 minute, then gradually blend in the milk, stirring continuously. Bring this sauce to the boil, season with salt and freshly ground pepper and simmer for 1-2 minutes. Take the pan off the heat and beat in the egg. (6) .... Place in the centre of a pre-heated oven and bake at 350°F, (180°C), gas Mark 4 for 35-40 minutes or until bubbling hot and browned. This is a rich and substantial meal, best served straight from the casserole. A tomato and onion salad may be served with it.

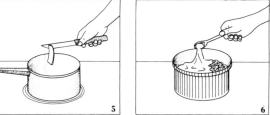

● Activity 3 — group work

Make up recipes for favourite dishes in your country.

13.3 Operating instructions

COMPACT STEREO CASSETTE RECORDER

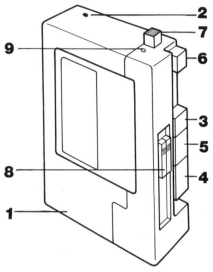

FEATURES

* Two headphone jacks are provided so that two of you can enjoy the music in private.
* The cue/review mechanism is handy for finding the start of tape programs and also for reviewing.
* The auto-stop mechanism automatically shuts down the player when the tape ends during playback.

PARTS AND THEIR FUNCTIONS

1 Battery Compartment
Insert 2 batteries here.

2 Headphone Jack (Stereo Mini-Jack)
Connect your headphones to this jack. Two jacks are provided so that you can connect two sets of headphones when listening to the sound together in private.

3 Fast-Forward/Cue Button
Press this down to fast-forward the tape. To skip some programs during playback, depress this button with the PLAY button pushed down.

4 Rewind/Review Button
Press this down to rewind the tape. To hear the same tape programs again during playback, depress this button with the PLAY button pushed down.

5 Play Button
Press this down to play back the tape.

6 Stop Button
Depress this to stop the tape.

7 Eject Button
Depress this to eject the tape.

8 Volume Controls
These adjust the sound heard through the headphones. The RIGHT control is for the right channel and the LEFT control is for the left channel. Use these controls to attain a balance in the sound through both channels.

9 'Operate' Lamp/Battery Check
This lamp lights while the cassette player is operating. It dims when the voltage level of the batteries drops.

LISTENING TO TAPES

1 Press the EJECT button to open the cassette lid and load the cassette.
2 Connect the accessory headphones.
3 Push down the PLAY button. Playback begins.
4 Adjust the balance in the left and right channel sound volume.
5 Depress the STOP button to stop the tape.
6 Open the cassette lid and depress the EJECT button to eject the tape.

● Activity 4

First, read the PARTS AND THEIR FUNCTIONS column, then join the numbers to their corresponding numbers on the diagram. Check that you have understood the function of each part.

● Activity 5 — pair work

Suppose you have given this cassette player as a present to a very impractical person, who misunderstands your explanations of the instructions. A list of his/her misunderstandings is given below. Correct them, referring to the instructions if necessary.

1 I can't use it when I'm moving about, then?
2 There's no way of adjusting the left and right sound independently, then?
3 If you press the STOP button, the cassette gets ejected automatically?
4 So you use this CUE button to wind back to the beginning?
5 So if there's a song I don't like and I want to skip to the next one, I have to stop the tape and then press the CUE button.

● Composition

1 Describe how to make either your favourite dish, or how to make a typical dish from your country.
2 Explain how you play your favourite game/sport. Explain the necessary techniques and/or the rules.
3 Explain how to do any do-it-yourself repair.
4 Imagine you have to explain your job to a person who is coming to take your place because you are leaving.

Persuasion

14

Checklist

● **Noun clauses**

What (the thing that) is good enough for the Queen is good enough for me. (**What** as subject)

Sparkle is **what** (the thing that) makes housewives' worries disappear. (As complement, after **to be**)

Sparkle is **what** (the thing that) you need. (As object)

The only thing that matters is love. (or: **What** matters, but NOT 'all what' or 'the only thing what'. **What** cannot be used with an adjective in front of it.)

All you need is love. (= the only thing (that) you need ...)

Everything salesmen say is aimed at making you buy something. (= **All the things** (that) salesmen say are aimed ..., but the first sentence is much more frequently found.)

It's amazing what children get up to. (= **What** children get up to is amazing, or: **The things that** children get up to are amazing.)

See Book 3, Exercise 17.

● **So, such and alternatives (1)**

It's **so nourishing**! (adjective) = **How nourishing** (it is)!

It's **such a** marvellous **car**! (noun) = **What a** marvellous **car**!

We don't really believe **such nonsense**. (uncountable noun) = **What nonsense**! We don't believe it.

See Book 3, Exercise 50C.

14.1 Buying and selling

● Dialogue 1

Janet has taken her son, Paul, 13, to buy some shoes. An assistant comes to help them.

Listen to the dialogue.

ASSISTANT Good afternoon, madam. Can I help you?

JANET Yes. I want some shoes for my son. Size $7\frac{1}{2}$, I think, but you never know at his age. They grow so fast.

ASSISTANT What kind of shoes are you looking for? Are they for school?

JANET Oh, yes. Black, with rubber soles. Otherwise, they wear out in no time. It's amazing what children get up to.

PAUL Why can't I get a pair of basketball boots, Mum, like Glenn?

JANET I know what's worrying you. All you're thinking about is playing football. It might stop you kicking your new shoes to pieces if you had to clean them, though.

ASSISTANT These are very reliable, hard-wearing shoes, madam. Size $7\frac{1}{2}$.

PAUL Oh, all right. They'll do.

JANET Try them on, Paul, and walk up and down in them. Are you sure they fit you? They're not too tight, are they?

ASSISTANT I think they might be too small for him in a few months' time. If I were you, Paul, I'd try an 8. You'll need a larger size before long.

● Dialogue 2

Louise and Martin have seen a new car in a showroom window. They go inside to enquire about it.

Listen to the dialogue.

MARTIN We were looking at the new Vampire in your window.

SALESMAN Yes, sir. Good morning, madam. Just look at the finish on the paintwork. Four coats of paint in all, corrosion-resistant. Would you like a closer look, sir? There are three models, of course. This is the GL 1500, the most expensive, but it's worth it for the extras. Would you like to sit down, madam? Very comfortable, isn't it? You have your stereo-cassette here, cigar lighter, the special picnic tray. The door mirrors work by remote control from this button here. No, they won't operate unless the engine's running, madam...

MARTIN Hm. How many miles does it do to the gallon?

SALESMAN Around 50* at cruising speed. In a built-up area, that would come down to 35** or so, of course.

LOUISE And how much does it cost?

SALESMAN Depending on the model, between five and six thousand. But that includes tax and you get free seat belts and so on.

MARTIN I see. Can we try it out?

SALESMAN Certainly. I'll arrange a test drive for you. Could you give me your name and address, sir?

* 50 miles per gallon = 5.6 litres per 100 kilometres
** 35 miles per gallon = 8 litres per 100 kilometres

● Activity 1 — role-play

Play the parts of a salesman/saleswoman and two customers buying:
1) a suit, a sweater and skirt, some sports clothes.
2) a washing machine, a television set, a camera.

● Dialogue 3

On TV, Trevor Grubb calls on Mrs June Arnold.

Listen to the dialogue.

TREVOR Good morning to Mrs June Arnold of Bristol. Mrs Arnold, you are one of the lucky housewives chosen to receive a free five-kilo drum of new violet Sparkle.

JUNE But I've never used Sparkle before. I've always used...

TREVOR Tch, tch, Mrs Arnold. Wait till you try Sparkle. Then you'll see the difference. And if you're not satisfied, we'll buy the drum back from you for £10.

(*A few days later.*)

TREVOR Well, good morning, June. How did you get on with Sparkle?

JUNE It's unbelievable! Look at my husband's shirts! Only new violet Sparkle could give them that whiteness. I'm convinced.

TREVOR Here's £10. We'll buy back what's left in the drum.

JUNE No, no. Now I've discovered Sparkle, I'm not going to let anyone take it away from me.

TREVOR That's what all housewives say. New violet Sparkle is what they need for an extra-white wash and they won't part with it at any price.

● Dialogue 4

In real life, Harold Monk calls on Mrs Judy Blake.

Listen to the dialogue.

HAROLD Good morning. Are you Mrs Judy Blake?

JUDY (*seeing the drum of Sparkle*) Not today, thank you.

HAROLD Mrs Blake, you're one of the lucky housewives chosen to receive a five-kilo drum of new violet Sparkle.

JUDY That's very nice of you, but I'd rather go on using what I've always used, thank you.

HAROLD It's a free offer, I assure you. If you don't find Sparkle better than what you're using now, we'll buy the drum back from you.

JUDY I don't really need it. Why is it violet, anyway?

HAROLD Well, it's, er...it contains a special ingredient, the ultra-violet whitener.

JUDY Oh, well, all right, I'll try it. How much will you give me for the drum if it doesn't work?

HAROLD £10, Mrs Blake, but I'm sure you'll be satisfied.

(*A few days later.*)

JUDY Ah, I've been waiting for you to arrive. £10, please. Look at my husband's shirts!

HAROLD But they're beautifully white, Mrs Blake. I don't see what....

JUDY Don't you? They were blue when I put them in the machine!

● Activity 2 — role-play

Try to sell your partner one of the following: some furniture polish, some cosmetics, an encyclopaedia, some brushes. Your partner should try to resist you. Then exchange roles for another product.

14.2 Advertising techniques

Advertisements appeal to people's secret wishes. Apart from saying a product is good, they emphasise people's basic human needs and anxieties. Most people want to be more attractive and better off than others, and they are afraid of being thought socially inferior and of being lonely. Advertisers flatter us but also appeal to our worst instincts: greed, snobbery and fear. That is why products are never 'cheap'; they are always 'not expensive', or they 'save money'. That is why we are asked to envy other people, and, by buying a product, to make them envy us. For this reason, most advertisements have an obvious message, but also a secondary one, contained in the combination of words and pictures.

SHE: I thought you were charming at the party, and when you picked me up tonight in that gleaming white Porsche, I half-expected that beautiful dinner, with the soft lights and the roses, but I still don't understand your secret. There's something subtle about you that makes you irresistible.

HE: (*thinks*) Strange that such an intelligent girl hasn't learnt the secret of Macho yet.

Macho is aftershave, about 97% alcohol. The obvious message is: if you wear Macho, girls will find you irresistible. The secondary message is: men who wear Macho drive Porsches and can afford to give their girlfriends flowers and expensive dinners.

● Activity 3

Look at the two advertisements below. The important words in the advertising copy have been emphasised to help you to decide how it is constructed. What is the obvious message of each advertisement? (What is it trying to sell?) What is the secondary message of the advertisement? What human weakness is it aiming at?

CAITHNESS PRIDE
· BEST WHISKY ·

Caithness Pride. **The ninth Duke of Caithness** would only drink **the best** whisky. So he built **his own private** still, in the **heart** of the Highlands, with the **fresh** water bubbling in the stream nearby. When we **acquired** the still, we **paid the Duke's heirs handsomely** for it. But it was worth it. After all, what was **good for the Duke** is too good to be kept a **secret.**

SAFEBURN

Planning a home demands **great care.** The fireplace should be **distinctive** and **elegant,** with a fire that looks like a fire, giving your family the **warmth** and **protection** they need.

Every year **7,000 people die in fires** in Britain, and hundreds of them are **little children.** Thousands more are **disfigured for life.**

When you choose a fire, choose Safeburn. It gives you the **atmosphere of home comfort** you are looking for, and **sets your mind at rest.**

● Activity 4

Below you can see the text of three advertisements (or 'commercials') shown on television, and the actors who were chosen to appear and speak the lines. As on page 83 decide what the obvious message of the commercials is and whether another message is contained in them. Why do you think these particular actors were chosen, and why are they dressed as they are in the pictures shown here? What image is the advertiser trying to project?

GETATAN.

Pale One. Good heavens, Sarah! Where did you get such
a beautiful tan at this time of year? Have
you been skiing in Switzerland?

Sarah. Well, I didn't go quite as far as that, actually.
(To viewers) I can hardly let her into the secret
now, can I? I didn't even leave home. A
Getatan Sun Bed will make you deliciously bronzed
in a week. If you don't get a tan in seven days,
you can ask for your money back. Why look pale
in winter? Get a Getatan!

NEWSPEAK.
Until I learned English with Newspeak, I was always tongue-
tied on holiday. I never realised how easy it was. For
only £3.80 a week, including the essential give-away
cassette, you too can speak English in only three months.
Twelve easy lessons, and no headaches next time you go
abroad. I've learned to make friends with Newspeak.

BONZO.
My dogs adore Bonzo. Chunks of nourishing meat, so full
of protein, with vitamin-rich liver. A treat for any dog!
When my dogs see me coming with Bonzo, their tails wag with
delight.

● Composition

1 What is the obvious message of the advertisements on pages 82–3?. Is there another message contained in them?
2 Do you think there should be any restrictions on advertisements in the newspapers or on television? If so, what should they be?
3 Write about an interview you had with someone trying to sell you something you did not really want.

Discussion:
Arguing for *and* against

Checklist

● **It and there**

There indicates the existence of something; **it** is used as a substitute construction for a subject.

It's a waste of money to invest in space exploration. (Investing/Investment in space exploration is a waste of money.)
It's not surprising that the article has aroused a great deal of sympathetic comment. (The fact that the article has aroused a great deal of sympathetic comment is not surprising.)
There should be a universal world language. (A universal world language should exist.)

It is followed by a **that** clause or infinitive after adjectives.

It's not surprising **that** the article has aroused comment.
It's easier (for teachers) **to** correct translations than **to** teach students to speak a foreign language.

Study Reference Section — **It's** + *adjective* + **for/that,** *page 146.*

● **One ... another; some ... others**

It is **one** thing to say that the exams we have should be improved; it is **another** to argue that we should do away with them altogether.
Some people come determined to make trouble; **others** do not.

● **Most (= the majority of)**

Most people do not have enough to eat.
Most of them had to stay at home and look after the kids.

● **Each, every, everyone, every other**

In each **case** (of the two I have mentioned) teachers are to blame. (In **every** case = In all cases)

Each can be used of more than two things, but they must be considered separately.

I think **everyone** (everybody) should be able to go to university. (**Everyone** means 'all the people', just as **everything** means 'all the things', but we prefer the single-word forms.)
My father used to take me to watch the local team **every other** Saturday. (= on alternate Saturdays)

15.1 Expressing opinion

● **Questionnaire**

How do you react to the opinions expressed in the questionnaire below? Mark your response by placing a tick (✓) in one of the columns provided.
How to answer the questionnaire:

+   I agree entirely.

+   I sympathise with the point of view, but there are a lot of other things that must be considered.

●   The statement misses the really important point in the argument. It's a meaningless simplification.

—   I don't agree, although I realise there is some truth in it.

—   I don't agree at all.

	+	+	●	—	—
1 People were a lot happier a hundred years ago.					
2 It's a waste of money to invest in space exploration.					
3 Men and women should be treated exactly the same.					
4 Football causes so much trouble that it should be banned.					
5 Exams prove nothing and should be abolished.					
6 There should be a universal world language taught in schools all over the world.					
7 Justice is really impossible since all lawyers are paid to obscure the truth.					
8 Everyone should have the opportunity of a university education.					
9 All the problems of the Third World countries are due to colonialism.					
10 Students should get on with their studies instead of getting involved in protests.					

● **Dialogues — 1**

Listen to these short dialogues. Notice how the second speaker either agrees or disagrees with the first.

URSULA Women are still discriminated against in most societies. They should have the same rights and opportunities as men.

+ DAVID I agree with you, of course, as far as the law is concerned, and I think that women should be paid the same as men for doing the same work. But the sexes are different, so they can't be treated exactly the same.

WENDY I think everyone should be able to go to university.

● STEVEN That's all right as far as it goes, but do you really mean everyone? I agree that everyone who wants to go and has the ability to take advantage of it should go, but it's wrong to think you can educate people against their will.

NICK Why don't these students get on with their work, instead of wasting their time and our money demonstrating?

– DIANE I haven't much sympathy with those who do nothing else, but you're not taking into account that they have a right to demonstrate and are probably more aware of what's wrong in society than a lot of older people.

● **Activity 1 — pair work**

It is difficult to accept or disagree with any of these statements without making an additional comment. Study the comments made in the previous conversations. Then take it in turns to read the statements. Respond appropriately, giving your own views.

● **Dialogue 2** [cassette icon]

Julie Arthur is talking to her grandfather.

Listen to the dialogue.

GRANDAD People were a lot happier when I was young.

JULIE Is that really true, Grandad? Our history teacher says there was a lot of unemployment and most people didn't have enough to eat.

GRANDAD Well, a lot of people were out of work in the 30s but we managed somehow. After all, things haven't changed all that much. There are a lot of people out of work now.

JULIE But they have social security now, don't they? And Miss Williams says it was worse in some parts of the country than others. Her father was a miner in Wales and they had a terrible time. The owner of the mine wouldn't let them into the mine to work. It was called a lock-out.

GRANDAD Hm, I don't suppose everyone was happier. It depends which people we're talking about.

JULIE And Miss Williams says her mother had to leave school at fourteen. She never had a chance of going to university. And girls had a hard life. Most of them just had to stay at home and look after the kids.

GRANDAD Well, I can't see much harm in that. It was a good thing your mother stayed at home till you went to school, wasn't it?

JULIE But Mum was happy when she got her old job back, and she didn't have to have eight or nine children she didn't want, as they did in your day.

GRANDAD Your grandmother didn't, either. Everyone didn't have as many children as that, you know. But on the whole you're probably right, Julie. People weren't really happier. What I meant was that they amused themselves more instead of looking at TV all evening without saying a word to anyone. Life was hard, but we enjoyed it. Now people never seem satisfied.

JULIE I know what you mean, Grandad. But maybe people are always the same, more or less, and when they get older they remember the good things so they think they were happier.

GRANDAD You've probably got it right, Julie. What I really meant, I suppose, was that people seemed a lot happier because *I* was young.

● **Activity 2 — pair work**

List the arguments Julie uses to modify Grandad's original statement and show how he gradually modifies his definition of happiness.

15.2 Developing a balanced argument

LETTERS

Let's Improve Exams not Abolish them

REFERENCE

Sir,

It is not surprising that the article published in your columns on February 8th, 'Down with Exams', has aroused a great deal of sympathetic comment among your readers. Everyone knows that examinations are frequently unsatisfactory. But when the author, Stephen Pratt,

REDEFINITION

concludes his argument by saying 'Exams prove nothing and should be abolished', he is surely confusing two issues. It is one thing to say that the exams we have should be improved; it is another to argue that we should do away with them altogether.

PERSONAL EXPERIENCE

As a teacher of French and Spanish, I am aware that the GCE 'O' level exam in these languages should be changed. At present, it requires only a reading knowledge of these languages, some evidence of writing ability, and above all the ability to translate into English. I agree

PARTIAL AGREEMENT

that it is hardly possible to judge a student's ability in a foreign language properly if you do not ask him/her to speak it or even listen to it. In the same way, most examinations in literature rely entirely on isolated prescribed books, instead of expecting students to study the work of writers as a whole and understand the

social background in which they wrote.

In each case, I suspect that teachers are partly to blame. It is much easier to prepare students by dictating set answers to likely questions on one Shakespeare play than to teach them to appreciate a number of plays. It is simpler to correct translations than to motivate students to express themselves in a foreign language. The exam system is seriously at fault because it encourages teachers to be lazy and makes them unwilling to experiment. Nevertheless, I do not believe that this means we should trust teachers and tutors at universities to award qualifications only on the basis of their personal opinion, as Mr Pratt suggests. I am sure my colleagues in the teaching profession are honest, but I, for one, would not like the sole responsibility of deciding my students' futures, and would not look forward to dealing with parents who would try to influence my judgement. Mr Pratt thinks no great harm would be done if people with an inadequate knowledge of foreign languages were allowed to pass. But would he like to be operated on by a surgeon who had gained his qualifications in a similar way?

David Ford, Exeter

REASONS

DISAGREEMENT

CONCLUSION

● **Activity 3**

Study the letter above. Note how the writer 1) defines the topic; 2) expresses sympathy for the point of view, using an example; 3) demonstrates the weakness of the solution proposed, using an example. Consider one of the statements made on page 86 in the questionnaire, and plan a similar answer. Does the statement need clarification? What else needs to be said to make a reasonable assessment of the problem? What intermediate solution can be proposed?

The article below is an answer to the point of view expressed in number 6 of the questionnaire on page 86, but the paragraphs and sentences are out of order.

Read the paragraphs separately and give each one a label from the following:
1 Reference to previous article.
2 Explanation of writer's main reason for different point of view.
3 His/her second reason for it.
4 The result of taking the opposite point of view.
5 Conclusion, suggesting a better course of action.

Put the paragraphs in the correct order 1-5. Now, taking each paragraph separately, rearrange the sentences into the most sensible order. (In the correctly reordered paragraphs 1 and 2 the first sentence is already in the correct position to help you.) You should now have a logically ordered argument.

3 a) No one doubts that it would be convenient if we all spoke the same language, but Ian Jefferson's article 'Compulsory Esperanto', in your last issue, avoids the whole question of the nature of language. b) It also ignores the inevitable objections that would be made to such a proposal on nationalistic grounds.

A compulsory universal language?

1 a) They may well choose English as an official means of communication for information purposes. b) That does not mean, however, that everyone will give up his own language and speak English instead. c) In fact, people are more likely to learn an existing language than an artificial one because different people have different needs.

4 a) This would imply that it was better than others, instead of simply being different. b) Mr Jefferson is in favour of Esperanto because he knows that people would naturally object to an existing language being made compulsory. c) Secondly, the proposal of an artificial language is in itself an admission of the difficulty of the problem.

2 a) Since people are inseparable from the language they speak, they would not communicate as much in Esperanto as in their own language in the family circle, and consequently are unlikely to adopt it. b) On the other hand, if we want to communicate on a friendly basis with people in another country there is no alternative to learning their language, just as we expect them to learn ours if they come to England. c) Apart from such questions of national pride, the result of Mr Jefferson's proposal would be the opposite of what he intends.

5 a) In the first place, language is not a code we can learn like a series of mathematical formulae. b) If you try to prevent people from speaking their own language and force them to use another, you limit their personalities, because no artificial language can express the range of meanings that have grown up over centuries in the languages of the world. (c) Languages develop naturally over the course of time as the means of expression of the people who speak them.

15.3 Reassessing the question

OPINION

BAN FOOTBALL

Cause or Effect

by Will Scott

After the incidents at a number of grounds last weekend the anti-football groups have once again called for a ban on professional matches in this country. For them, the issue is clear. Violence on the field causes violence on the terraces and in the streets, and if we stop football, we will prevent the violence.

No one hates violence more than I do, but I suspect that the people who advocate such a drastic solution are in danger of confusing cause with effect, and are really blaming football clubs for the ills of modern society.

Unlike the majority of these people, I have been a football fan since I was a boy of seven or eight and my father used to take me to watch the local team every other Saturday. In those days there were only two or three policemen to look after a crowd of 20,000 people. Now there are a whole army of them, with squad cars, Alsatian dogs and walkie-talkie radios, to keep half that number in order.

Under these circumstances, it is not surprising that psychologists and sociologists want to ban football altogether. But I don't think these experts have attended many football matches recently. The fact is that the phenomenon in Britain is very different from what it is abroad. What the experts, and most foreigners, cannot understand is that it isn't the match or the result that produces the violence. They suppose that spectators get angry because their team is losing, and, in many countries, violence does tend to be directed at the referee or the visiting team. But in Britain some people, whichever team they say they support, come determined to make trouble, whatever the result.

Football is an exciting game. I find myself shouting for the team I support as loudly as anyone else and am willing to believe for a few moments that the referee is blind and the other team are villains. But everyone behaved like that 30 years ago, when there was just as much violence on the pitch, but very little off it. The truth of the matter is that football is played at the weekend, when young thugs have nothing else to do, and it provides them with an excuse for mindless violence. If we closed all the football grounds tomorrow, the violence would go on somewhere else.

It is no use blaming football clubs for what happens. Most of them spend money they cannot afford hiring the police to keep order. Violence in our society is something we have to cure but its roots have very little to do with football.

● **Activity 5 — pair work**

Read through the newspaper article above. Then re-read the paragraphs separately and give each one a suitable label or heading. Compare your labels, then take it in turns to summarise the content of each paragraph in your own words.

● **Composition**

1 Write a composition on any of the topics listed on page 86 where you have responded ●, except 1, 4, 5 and 6. Plan a heading for each paragraph to help you order your argument clearly.

2 If you disagree with the arguments put forward in this unit on topics 1, 4, 5 and 6, write, stating your reasons. Plan a heading for each paragraph to help you order your argument clearly.

Reacting to possible circumstances

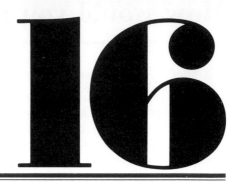

Checklist

● **Conditional sentences (2)**

The following model sentences are hypothetical. They relate to imaginary situations in present time or in the future. The conditional clause, which can come first or second, takes the Past form, while the other clause takes the Conditional (**would**). **If I/he/she/it were** is formally correct, but **was** is becoming increasingly common in such sentences.

If I **were** (was) rich, I **would buy** a yacht.
If I **had** a lot of money, I **would buy** a house.
If I **had to** work as hard as you, I **would change** my job.

See Book 3, Exercise 98A.

● **Either ... or, neither ... nor**

If I won a million pounds, I would have a long holiday abroad, **either** in India **or** in Japan.
I would**n't** go to India **or** Japan (either).
I would **neither** go to India **nor** to Japan. (Very formal, and most unusual in conversation)
I would**n't** go to India.
— **Neither** (**Nor**) **would I**. (Notice the inversion here: **would I**.)

● **Enough**

If I were **lucky enough** to win a million pounds, I'd give the money away. (**Enough** comes after an adjective.)
I would give some of it away, but I'd keep **enough money** to live on. (**Enough** comes before a noun.)
I don't know him **well enough** to recommend him. (**Enough** comes after an adverb.)

See Book 3, Exercises 33A—B.

● **Are you a good survivor — Psychologically?**

Complete this light-hearted test to find out whether you are likely to cope with possible problems in the future. Choose what you would probably do in the following circumstances. Check your score on page 163.

Are You a Good Survivor —Psychologically?

Complete this light-hearted test to find out whether you are likely to cope with possible problems in the future. Choose what you would probably do in the following circumstances.

1 If you were in a department store and people said there was a bomb there, would you a) run towards the door? b) keep calm and follow the directions given to get out? c) start to organise everyone else?

2 If you had to stay in bed for a month, would you a) be impatient until you could get up? b) suffer in silence? c) relax and read?

3 If there was a bakers' strike, would you a) eat other things? b) start making your own bread? c) fill the fridge with enough bread for a week and hope the strike would end before your supplies ran out?

4 If your new sweater shrank the first time you wore it, would you a) take it back and complain angrily? b) complain firmly but calmly? c) prefer not to complain?

5 If your mother-in-law asked to stay with you for the third time in six months would you a) make her welcome? b) accept her unwillingly? c) refuse?

6 If you overheard two people saying unkind things about you, would you a) confront them? b) forget about it? c) say nothing, but worry?

7 If you had the chance of making a lot of money on the stock market, would you a) gamble, and enjoy it? b) gamble, and worry? c) not take the risk?

8 If your company closed down, would you a) make realistic plans for the future? b) rely on social security? c) think of alternative skills you could develop to get another job?

9 If you were involved in a car accident, would you a) take the blame? b) blame the other person? c) keep calm and find witnesses?

10 If a friend asked your advice on a personal matter, would you a) listen sympathetically? b) start giving him/her advice with confidence? c) feel you hadn't time to listen to it all?

● Are you like your sun sign?

Do you know your astrological sign? This chart will tell you what typical members of that sign are like, and help you to decide how they would react to the questionnaire opposite.

● Activity 1

Choose any three signs that interest you, and decide how these people would answer the questionnaire. Turn to page 163 to find out if your own answers are typical of your sign.

ARIES
(21st March-20th April)

Characteristics: energy, courage, decisiveness, tactlessness, impatience, selfishness. You would be good in emergencies, willing to gamble, or find another job. But you wouldn't be patient with other people or likely to save money.

TAURUS
(21st April-21st May)

Characteristics: calm, common sense, practical skill, inability to adapt to new situations. You would make bread and save money but wouldn't like your plans to be changed.

GEMINI
(22nd May-21st June)

Characteristics: adaptability, versatility, fluency in speaking, indecision, a lack of practical skills. You'd easily find another job and talk your way out of trouble, but you wouldn't enjoy dealing with household problems.

CANCER
(22nd June-22nd July)

Characteristics: thrift, adaptability, household management, tendency to worry and be sensitive to criticism. You would be kind to relations, would make bread, but wouldn't be good in a sudden emergency, and wouldn't like gambling.

LEO
(23rd July-22nd August)

Characteristics: self-confidence, ability to organise, optimism, all of which can go too far. You'd be perfect in a crisis, and speak fluently. Better at gambling than saving.

VIRGO
(23rd August-22nd September)

Characteristics: common sense, efficiency, adaptability, but too proud of efficiency and lacking in confidence in other things. You'd solve the practical problems easily, and be good in an emergency, unless it involved risks or appearing in public.

LIBRA
(23rd September-22nd October)

Characteristics: charm, kindness to others, reasonable attitudes, indecision. You would apologise beautifully and complain tactfully, but saving money would be difficult, and an emergency would worry you.

SCORPIO
(23rd October-22nd November)

Characteristics: courage, determination, inflexibility, resentment of injustice or injury. A good survivor in most circumstances, you wouldn't like being inconvenienced.

SAGITTARIUS
(23rd November- 22nd December)

Characteristics: cheerfulness, good in emergencies, tactlessness, not good in the house. You would handle most things well, but might say the wrong thing in some situations.

CAPRICORN
(23rd December- 20th January)

Characteristics: practical ability, common sense, calm, intolerance, pessimism. You would solve the practical problems and put up with inconvenience, but problems in the future would worry you.

AQUARIUS
(21st January-18th February)

Characteristics: coolness, detachment, separation from events. You wouldn't mind doing without bread and you could handle people in most situations without losing your temper.

PISCES
(19th February-20th March)

Characteristics: sensitivity, adaptability, indecisiveness, willingness to accept what others say. You would be kind to relations, sympathetic to friends, but you would not have enough self-confidence to take charge in an emergency.

16.2 What would you do?

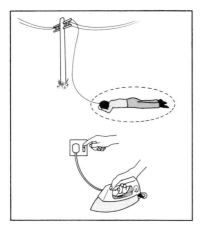

Electric shock

Injuries caused by electric shock are fairly common. When a person has received a shock from a high-voltage cable and has not been thrown clear, no one should approach him/her until the current has been turned off. If a shock occurring at work or at home causes someone to lose consciousness, electrical contact must be broken before anyone attempts to give assistance. You should either switch off the appliance at the mains or, if that is not possible, push the victim away with a dry piece of wood.

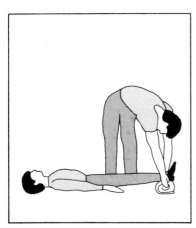

Treatment of shock

Look out for signs of shock. People who have been injured or who may have lost a lot of blood, or those who have had heart attacks, may be in deep shock. The signs to look for are faintness, paleness, a moist, sticky skin, shallow, rapid breathing and a fast but weak pulse rate.

Shock can prove fatal, and it is essential to do something to prevent its developing. The best way to treat or prevent shock is to keep the patient lying down, preferably with the legs higher than the head; if possible, raise the lower part of the body on a rolled-up packet or similar object. Make the patient as comfortable as possible, loosening any tight clothing, and reassure him/her because fright increases the effects of shock. Do not give hot, sweet tea or anything by way of mouth, since fluid swallowed may be vomited, and, if the person is injured or unconscious, flow back into the windpipe. Do not try to heat the victim with hot water bottles and heavy blankets, either. Overheating dilates the blood vessels of the skin and draws blood away from the organs inside the body that need this blood in an emergency. These traditional first-aid practices are potentially dangerous.

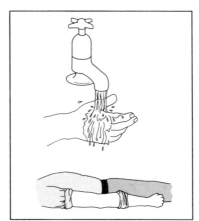

Burns and scalds

Burns caused by dry heat and scalds caused by moist heat are treated similarly. The aim is to cool the skin as fast as possible. Skin damage often occurs after help has arrived because tissues are still very hot. The first thing to do is to tear or cut clothes off as quickly as possible. Lay the casualty down and cool the burn by immersing it in cold water for at least ten minutes; if the patient is suffering from shock, he/she should lie down with his/her legs raised.

No creams or ointments should be used. All that is necessary is to cover the damaged area of skin with a clean dressing such as a sheet or tablecloth.

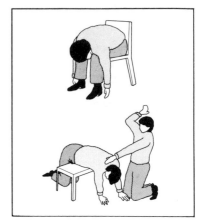

Fainting and choking

Fainting is caused by a failure of the blood supply to the brain. The victim should lie down or sit on a chair, legs apart and head down, and then sit up after a few minutes. Repeat this process if necessary. Loosen tight clothing round the neck, the chest and the waist.

If an adult is choking, lean him/her over a table and slap him/her hard between the shoulder blades. Do not try to remove an object with your fingers. A child should be held upside down and slapped on the back.

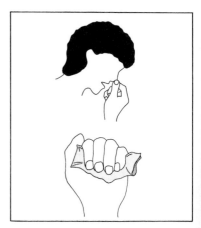

Haemorrhage

Controlling a haemorrhage is an important part of first aid. Most nose bleeds can be controlled by getting the patient to sit up and squeezing the soft part of the nose between finger and thumb until the bleeding stops. You can control bleeding from the palm of the hand by squeezing a clean pad of handkerchief tightly in the fist and applying continuous pressure to the place that is bleeding.

● First aid quiz

Here are some questions on first aid. Most, but *not all* of the information you require is in the text. When you have chosen your answer, explain what would happen if you did the *wrong* thing. You can check your answers on page 163.

1 If you had to treat an unconscious person who had just received an electric shock from a live wire or cable and had not been thrown clear, would you
  A turn off the current and approach to pull him/her clear?
  B pull him/her clear as quickly as possible?

2 If you had to treat a person who had fainted, would you
  A make the patient stand up as soon as possible and move about to get the blood circulation moving?
  B make the patient lie or sit down with legs apart and head down?

3 After a few minutes, would you make him/her
  A sit up?
  B walk about?

4 If you had to deal with a person who had just been burnt or scalded, would you
  A rub in cream or ointments on the affected skin?
  B immerse the affected parts in cold water?

5 If you had to deal with a person who was bleeding from a bad cut, would you
  A put a tight bandage (tourniquet) above the cut?
  B press firmly for at least ten minutes at the place where the blood was coming out?

6 If you had to treat a child who was choking, would you
  A hold him/her upside down and slap him/her on the back?
  B try to remove the object causing the choking, with your fingers?

7 If you had to deal with a person suffering from shock (e.g. after an accident) would you
  A give him/her a warm drink and wrap him/her up in blankets?
  B keep the person lying down and avoid giving him/her food or drink?

8 What would you tell a person who was suffering from shock following a bad accident?
  A There's been a terrible accident. All your friends are dead, and you've been lucky to escape.
  B The ambulance is just coming. Don't worry.

16.3 Using your imagination

Use your imagination — but don't get carried away!

by Clive Morrison

The English mistress at school was fond of asking us to write compositions on hypothetical subjects. 'They help you to use your imagination,' she used to say. So she would pick topics like: *What would you do if you won a million pounds on the football pools?* Mike O'Hara, the joker of the class, wrote: 'I'd probably die of shock,' and had to do extra work for not taking the question seriously. Another favourite was: *Where would you go if you were offered a free holiday anywhere in the world?* This produced some remarkable fantasies, complicated by our limited knowledge of geography. Someone wanted to cross the Andes on a camel! And then there was the cultural fantasy: *If you were wrecked on a desert island, which three books (or records) would you take with you, and why?* Mike asked if he could take three film stars, and Miss Collett wouldn't allow it. She was exercising censorship in advance. She knew him well enough to realise he wasn't going to take John Wayne, Gary Cooper and Humphrey Bogart!

It is amazing how long some of these daydreams still endure in people's lives. Every week a few million people post their pools coupons in the hope of winning a fortune and it is interesting that more people take part if there was a big win the week before.

It is much easier than it used to be to have holidays where you like, and there are advertisements in the newspapers inviting you to cross the Sahara, go over the Himalayas and walk along the Great Wall of China. On the other hand, most people unfortunate enough to be shipwrecked are too busy trying to survive to pack their favourite books or remember to take the hi-fi with them, and anyway, there are not so many uninhabited islands left.

The urge to get away from the pressures of modern life exists, however, and the average man's idea of this kind of paradise is probably still close to that of the tenth-century Persian poet, Omar Khayyam: 'A jug of wine, a loaf of bread and Thou beside me, singing in the wilderness'. I'm not sure if the average woman would vote for that. After all, who would make the next loaf of bread? Not Omar, you can be sure. Besides, I can think of one woman who would say: 'You? Singing? Not likely! I'd rather drown!'

● **Activity 2**

Discuss your answers to Miss Collett's questions with other members of the class.

● **Composition**

1 What would you do if you won a large sum of money — enough to stop work if you wanted to?

2 Where would you go if you were offered a month's holiday for two or more people anywhere in the world? What would you do there?

3 If you were wrecked on a desert island, which three objects would you take with you from the ship? Do you think you would survive and, if so, how?

Narrative: Speculation, deduction and turning points

17

Checklist

This unit concentrates on narratives where people wonder what may have happened, or decide what must have happened, and consider what would have happened if something else had taken place. The main structures necessary are the past forms of modals, and the third Conditional.

Study Reference Section — Modals, page 149.

● **May (possibility), might (less likely possibility), must (deduction), can't and couldn't (impossibility)**

ANNE The phone's ringing. It **may be** Joan.
JUDY It **might be**, but she phoned half an hour ago.
ANNE Then it **must be** Angela.
JUDY It **can't be** (**couldn't be**). She's in Australia.
ANNE Well why don't you answer it, and find out?

Suppose the phone rang while Anne was in the bath, and she couldn't answer it. Judy was out. The conversation when Judy came home would then be:

ANNE The phone rang while you were out. It **may have been** Joan.
JUDY It **might have been**, but I saw her this afternoon.
ANNE Then it **must have been** Angela.
JUDY It **can't have been** (**couldn't have been**). She's in Australia. Anyway, why didn't you answer it, and find out?

● **Needn't and mustn't**

You **needn't** worry. (It's unnecessary, there's no reason to.)
You **mustn't** worry. (Don't worry. It's bad for you.)
You **needn't have** worried. (There was no reason to worry, but you did.)
I **didn't need to** worry. (There was no reason to worry, so I didn't.)

Study Reference Section — Modals, page 149. See Book 3, Exercise 53B.

● **Conditional sentences (3)**

The third Conditional refers to the past and says what would have/might have happened if the situation had been different.

The clause containing **if** is in the Past Perfect (**had** + past participle); the other clause is the Conditional Perfect (**would have** + past participle).

If I **had seen** him, I **would have told** him about it. (I didn't see him.)
If I **hadn't known** who he was, I **wouldn't have recognised** him. (I did know who he was.)

17.1 Speculation and deduction

● **Dialogue** 🔲

It is three o'clock on a Sunday morning in winter. Russell and Isabel are still up. They are waiting for their teenage children, Tracy and Nick, to come home from a party.

Listen to the dialogue.

RUSSELL Do you realise what time it is, Isabel?

ISABEL Yes. Bedtime.

RUSSELL It's three o'clock. And those two aren't back yet.

ISABEL They must be enjoying themselves.

RUSSELL But they said they'd be back by half-past one.

ISABEL Well, you know what it's like at parties, dear. You can't expect them to watch the clock. It must have gone on longer than they expected. They may have met some interesting people. They'll be back soon. Don't worry.

RUSSELL Nick said the party would be over by one o'clock at the latest. What do you think can have happened to them?

ISABEL They must be on their way by now.

RUSSELL I don't like it, Isabel! It's snowing, and the roads are dangerous. They may be in trouble. They might even have had an accident! I don't know how you can take things so calmly. For all we know, our children may be lying in hospital right now!

ISABEL Oh, really, Russell! You must realise that they're grown up. You needn't worry so much, honestly.

RUSSELL Well, I can't help it. Who have they gone with, anyway?

ISABEL You know who they've gone with — Frankie and Alice.

RUSSELL Frankie and Alice! You can't have let them go with Frankie driving! He's my idea of disaster on wheels! Surely you can't have forgotten the time when he crashed into the back of me!

ISABEL Well, I'm sure he must have improved since then. Anyway, it seemed all right to me. And I couldn't lend them my car. The brakes need seeing to. They might have had an accident.

RUSSELL Ah, you're admitting now that that's a possibility!

(*The phone rings.*)

ISABEL That must be them now. (*She goes out to answer it.*)

RUSSELL It may be. It may be the police. It might even be the hospital!

ISABEL (*coming back*) Well, you needn't have worried, dear. They're staying the night at Frankie and Alice's. Aren't we lucky to have such sensible children? Are you coming to bed?

● **Activity 1 — role-play**

Look at the following situations. Then work in pairs, with one of you as a 'pessimist' (like Russell in the dialogue) and the other as an 'optimist', to make up the possible dialogues the situations might produce.

1 The pessimist has lost his/her keys. The optimist suggests possible places where they might be: **You may/might have...** The pessimist answers negatively with: **No, I can't have left them there, because...** until he/she reaches a logical conclusion: **I must have left ...**

2 Until recently, a teacher said you were the best group he/she had ever had, but now he/she is criticising you more.

3 Recently a friend's behaviour towards you has changed completely.

4 Until recently, a middle-aged single man/woman who lives near you used to go around with a long face, but now he/she always seems to be happy.

5 Some friends of yours have gone to live in a more expensive area of town, and now it seems they don't want to know you.

● Activity 2

Look at the following picture contrasts.
Working in pairs, suggest reasons for the
changed attitudes of the people in 1 and 2,
and for the non-arrival of your friends in 3.

BEFORE

NOW

The boss you both work for was always bad-tempered and
very demanding.

He is behaving very differently — kind, considerate,
understanding.

You often have a coffee together at a cafe near your
language school. The waitress used to be happy and
smiling.

She is always bad-tempered.

Some friends are away on holiday abroad, and asked you to
meet them at the airport.

The plane has arrived, but they were not on it and the
airline says their names were not on the list of passengers.

17.2 Turning points

Ray Charles

Ray Charles was born on September 23rd 1930 into a poor family in Georgia, U.S.A. His father was a railwayman who had to travel a lot, so Ray was brought up mainly by his mother, who, though not very well educated, was full of common sense.

TURNING POINT 1: He goes blind

When he went blind with glaucoma at the age of seven, it was his mother who helped him to face up to the situation. She told him he was blind, not stupid, and that he had lost his eyes but not his mind; she made him sweep floors and chop wood to show him he was by no means helpless. She used to tell him that some day she would not be there to help him, and that then he would have to look after himself. Thanks to her training he was able to understand that if he thought long enough about something, he would almost always find a way of doing it by himself.

Soon after he went blind, Ray began to take an interest in music. A neighbour

TURNING POINT 2: He develops a talent for music

showed him how to play simple tunes on the piano, and he had a love for the slow hymns he heard played and sung in the local church. By the time he began to attend the blind school he had developed a passion and talent for music, and the schoolteachers encouraged him to study a variety of instruments. Then, one more blow came. His mother, who was still only in her early thirties, died suddenly, and Ray, who loved her deeply, was so shocked that for two weeks he was unable to eat. It was another neighbour who finally managed to persuade him that his mother would have wanted him to go on,

and reminded him of how she had believed in him. When his father died a year later, Ray knew he was strong enough to keep going on his own.

Between the ages of fifteen and seventeen, Ray worked with bands in Florida, but in 1948, while still only seventeen, he decided that there wasn't much future for him there and asked a friend to help him choose a new place to go to. They eventually chose Seattle, in the north-west of the U.S.A.

TURNING POINT 3 He leaves Florida

Ray arrived in Seattle after a five-day bus journey and went to a small hotel to sleep. When he woke up, 21 hours later, he was hungry, it was two o'clock in the morning, and everywhere was closed, but the hotel receptionist sent him to a small after-hours club where they sometimes served food. Ray managed to find the place and knocked on the door. A man on the door said they had no food, but 'We've got a talent night on here,' he added. Ray saw his chance and told the man he could play the piano and sing. The man tried to discourage him, but he was eventually guided to the piano and sang a song called 'Driftin' Blues'. As he came off the stand, a man stopped him and said, 'I'm from the Elks Club. Get yourself a trio and you've got a weekend job.' That was Tuesday. By Friday he was working regularly, and after that he never looked back. It was the beginning of his climb to stardom.

TURNING POINT 4 He gets his big opportunity in Seattle.

● Activity 3

Look at the four main turning points in Ray Charles's early life. What do you think might have happened if:

1 it hadn't been for his mother's training (when he went blind)?
2 he hadn't developed his talent for music?
3 he hadn't left Florida?
4 he hadn't found the job in Seattle?

Think of 4 or 5 possibilities in each case.

● Composition

1 Write a letter to a friend, explaining what you felt when someone you are fond of came home very late one night last week, and how the situation was eventually resolved happily.
2 Write a composition on the life of Ray Charles, indicating the turning points in his life and what might otherwise have happened to him.
3 Think of turning points in your own life, and explain how your life might have been different if they had not happened.

Prescribed books: Characters

Checklist

● **Word order of adjectives**

1 Adjectives always come before the noun.
2 **And** should only be used to join adjectives when they appear as a complement, not before a noun; if there are three adjectives or more, **and** appears between the second-to-last one and the last.

He was **determined**. He was **a determined man**.
She was **single-minded and persistent**.
She had **a single-minded, persistent attitude** to her work.
He seemed **youthful, modern and up to date**.
He had **a youthful, modern, up-to-date outlook** on life.

Study Reference Section — Adjectives: word order, page 145.
See Book 3, Exercise 18.

● **Purpose clauses (2)**

See Unit 9.

So that is required when there is a change of subject from one clause to the next.

He left some money in his will **to give** his nephew a good education.
He left some money in his will **so that** his nephew **would have** a good education. (**would be given** a good education)
Advertisers prefer people to watch rubbish on television **to prevent** them **from thinking about** reality.
Advertisers prefer people to watch rubbish on television **so that** they **will not think about** reality.

See Book 3, Exercises 44A—D.

● **because and because of**

Sherlock Holmes is a successful creation **because** Conan Doyle **chose** Dr Watson as the narrator.
Sherlock Holmes is a successful creation **because of the choice** of Dr Watson as the narrator.

18.1 Historical figures

● **Were they like their sun sign?**

Napoleon Bonaparte

Winston Churchill

1 Undoubtedly he was **practical** and **a good businessman**, as well as being **artistic**. He made money, saved it and invested it. But he wrote 37 plays in twenty years, which suggests he was not **lazy**, and was always willing to try something new, so he was not **inflexible**, either. Leaving your wife at the age of twenty is not the sign of a **possessive** man, but his love poems make it clear that he was **affectionate**.

2 She was called the Virgin Queen, which seems appropriate, though most women with her sign **get married**! She was not **modest**, but she was **diplomatic**. She had a **calculating, analytical** mind. She may have **worried too much**, but she had a terrible temper, which is not typical, and she was mean, which is not typical, either. She was herself.

3 At first sight, he seemed above all a **youthful, modern, up-to-date** personality, **lively** and **spontaneous** in his behaviour and **full of nervous energy**. All politicians have to be **adaptable**, and he was **highly intelligent**, too. Since his death, some reports have suggested he was **unreliable** in his affections and **inconsistent**.

4 She was **determined** and she must have been **ambitious**, although she seemed **humble**. But she wasn't very **prudent** and we don't know if she had **a sense of humour**. She was a **disciplined** soldier, but no one could imagine her as **mean, conventional** or **pessimistic**. Her faith in God was no doubt too strong for her to have had these failings.

5 He always seemed **optimistic, good-humoured** and **larger than life**. He had **a tendency to exaggerate** and many people thought him **tactless** and **irresponsible**, but he was also remarkably **perceptive**. He was **frank** and **sincere**, and could be very **witty**. When a lady said that if she were his wife, she would poison his coffee, he replied, 'Madam, if *you* were my wife, I would drink it.'

Henry VIII

Sarah Bernhardt

William Shakespeare

6 He had **a strong sense of purpose**, in his case identified with nationalism, and his **powerful feelings and emotions** also came to be devoted to this end. As a young man, he had an **imaginative** approach to military questions, and throughout his career he was **single-minded, persistent** and **determined**. If he seemed **jealous, suspicious** and **secretive**, these characteristics were part of his national pride, too.

7 He was **a pioneer** in his field and **adventurous** technically. He must have been **energetic**, too; he made so many films. Most actors are **selfish** or at least **self-centred**, but as a director he was not **impulsive** or **quick-tempered**. He was, above all, **witty** and **satirical** and he loved freedom. That is why he made *The Great Dictator*.

Frédéric Chopin

8 He doesn't seem to have been very **generous**. His armies never paid for what they took. But he was **creative** and **intelligent**, **a born leader** and **great organiser**, with **a liking for self-dramatisation**. He was **broad-minded**, certainly **hungry for power** and **conceited**, but he had reason to be **proud** of his achievements.

9 He had the reputation of an **idealistic, humanitarian, progressive** reformer. He was **independent** in his views, **quick-witted** and when he was young, **unpredictable**. His married life was **unconventional** and even a little **perverse** — he preferred his wife's sister to his wife!

Joan of Arc

John F Kennedy

Elizabeth I

10 Something seems wrong here. She had **great charm**, but she was strong-minded, not **indecisive**, hot-tempered, not **calm and balanced**, very self-assured and not **easily influenced**. Probably all actresses are **changeable**, but few of them **love harmony** and are **selfless** enough to sacrifice themselves to avoid quarrels for the good of others.

11 Listening to his music, you imagine a **sensitive, emotional, gentle** man, like many romantic artists **not worldly**, and **not very practical**. In some of his relationships he was **weak-willed**, but he was patriotic as well as **adaptable**, and not only an **intuitive** genius but a technical master of his craft.

Charles de Gaulle

12 A **kind, sensitive, sympathetic** person? No, that's not him! If having six wives means you are **home-loving**, he was, and executing two of them shows he was **jealous**. He was **fond of money** (but spent it, which is untypical), **moody** and **changeable**. He had most of the vices of the sign but few of the virtues.

Charles Dickens

Charlie Chaplin

● Activity 1 — group work

The above descriptions are of the twelve famous historical figures illustrated on these two pages. Each one was born under a different sign of the zodiac, and the adjectives in bold type are supposed to be characteristic of their sun sign.

1 Match the descriptions with the people in the pictures. Check your answers with those given on page 164.
2 See if you can recognise yourself as a combination of any of the groups of adjectives. Check on page 93 to see if you are like your sun sign.
3 Find appropriate adjectives to describe the characters in the novel or play you are reading.

103

18.2 Character and type

● **Victorian melodrama**

Victorian melodrama expresses the conventional idea of character in its simplest form. Where else can we find heroes who are so noble, heroines who are so innocent, and villains who are so diabolically evil? The minor characters are stereotypes, too. Fathers are either inflexible tyrants or benevolent old men; mothers are saintly. The hero usually has a close friend, an honest, trustworthy confidant. The heroine is more likely to be alone, so that the author can emphasise her innocence and vulnerability.

The conventions of these plays reflected social changes. The country was always good, the city wicked, because most of the audience had been forced to look for work in towns during the Industrial Revolution and liked to feel nostalgic about 'the good old days'. In the crowded, insanitary conditions of the cities children often died, and most melodramas included pitiful, innocent creatures who were eventually allowed to die after the author had extracted the last drop of sentiment from their plight. The villains were upper- or middle-class, dishonest landowners or businessmen who exploited their employees, or crooked lawyers, but melodrama never attempted social criticism. Individuals might be wicked, but the system was never challenged.

Melodramas nearly always had a happy ending. They were close enough to the grim reality of the audience's lives to enable them to identify with the characters, who were suitably exaggerated to make them instantly recognisable. But at the same time ugly facts were transformed into a kind of fairyland of wish-fulfilment. Somehow, virtue always triumphed and the wicked were punished, either because of an improbable coincidence, like a rich uncle appearing from Australia, or, even more improbably, because the wicked repented.

The endless family sagas imported these days from the United States show that the principles of melodrama are still in operation, even though tastes have changed. The consumer society — and these serials, after all, are paid for by advertising — has made most of the characters richer. Their fast cars, swimming pools and elegant homes are another kind of wish-fulfilment. The heroine is no longer dressed simply; her clothes reflect the aspirations of the working-class girls who watch the serial. She is not so innocent, either; we have rejected Victorian ideas about sex. The picture of life is as false as it always was, however. This is because melodrama exists so that people will not think about reality. It is a way of allowing them to enjoy their daydreams, and, in its way, understandable. Most people have had enough of reality after listening to the world news!

● **Activity 2**

Consider the characters in the novel or play you are reading. Are they individuals (real characters)? If so, what makes them individual? Or are they types? Where else have you come across similar types in books or films?

● Famous detectives

Study the short descriptions of famous detectives given below. In each case, the writer is using a different technique to try to explain the essential characteristics of the detective's appeal to the public.

Philip Marlowe (Raymond Chandler)

Marlowe is tough, good-looking and popular with women, but what makes him so much more entertaining than other detectives of this type is his sense of humour. In one novel, Marlowe is about to be beaten up by a gangster when an enormous policeman appears, knocks him out, and, without saying anything, goes into a restaurant for dinner. The gangster, holding his jaw, says, 'That's Big Willy. He thinks he's tough.' 'You mean he's not sure,' Marlowe remarks, looking down at him.

Sherlock Holmes (Sir A. Conan Doyle)

Holmes interests us because of his powers of deduction. He solves mysteries by logic and observation, and the stories appeal to us in the same way as a good game of chess. But Conan Doyle also gave him a number of personal characteristics that make him human, not a machine — his love of music, for example, and his ability to disguise his face and voice. Above all, Holmes is a successful creation because of the choice of Dr Watson, his straightforward, rather simple-minded friend, as narrator. This means that Holmes's deductions seem even cleverer because they always come as a surprise to the reader, as well as to Watson.

Maigret (Georges Simenon)

Maigret is the opposite of James Bond on the one hand and Hercule Poirot on the other. Bond is a violent snob, a connoisseur of wine, food and women, who always tells us where he buys his clothes and guns. Maigret is happily married, conscious of his humble social origins, and lives on beer and sandwiches. Poirot is a comic Belgian (comic to English people, perhaps!), who solves murders by some kind of amateur psychology, but for Agatha Christie murder is a game you play after dinner, and the ten or fifteen suspects are all stereotypes. Maigret uses patient investigation and a deep understanding of human nature. Above all, Simenon — a real Belgian — made him the personification of justice, not the justice of the law, but a human ideal of justice that is infinitely more satisfying.

● Activity 3

Find examples of the writer's use, in the first passage above, of quotation to prove his argument; in the second, of examples in the third, of comparison.

18.3 Character and theme

Jay Gatsby and the American Dream

Scott Fitzgerald's reputation depends primarily on his portrayal of the 1920s, the age he is identified with, which he himself called 'The Jazz Age'. *The Great Gatsby* is such a fine novel that we cannot do justice to it simply as an account of the times Fitzgerald lived in, but it is certainly true that the atmosphere he creates of the rich, dancing and drinking at Gatsby's fabulous parties, fixes that period in the United States in our imagination.

Nevertheless, the novel symbolises far more than a society frantically determined to have a good time, and Gatsby, the enigmatic hero, is clearly intended to be much more than a gangster or a poor boy who has somehow made a fortune. No doubt he is ruthless in business—we never really find out what he does—but he is also a romantic. His love for Daisy, the girl he met during the First World War, has not altered in spite of her marriage to Tom Buchanan, the typical representative of the ruling classes. He has built his house so that he can see the green light of the Buchanans' dock across the water, and his

parties are intended to impress Daisy with his newly-acquired wealth and social connections. Above all, he believes that you can turn back the clock, that you can recapture the innocence of first love.

Nick Carraway, the narrator, gives Gatsby enormous significance before we even meet him. Gatsby, he tells us, 'had an extraordinary gift for hope'. When Gatsby is eventually

killed by a jealous husband, whose real victim should have been Tom Buchanan, and all his former guests desert him at the funeral, Carraway remembers that he once told him, 'You're better than the whole lot of them.'

The critic, Lionel Trilling, pointed out that Gatsby stands for the United States itself. He is a self-made man who has come from humble origins by means of hard work and business tactics that are often dubious, but he retains a romantic ideal in spite of his experience. Trilling suggests that Americans themselves often strike foreigners in this way.

In the great concluding paragraphs of the novel, Fitzgerald confirms Trilling's analysis. Carraway reflects that Gatsby's dream of happiness with Daisy is like the American dream that the future will be bright and new. Unlike Gatsby, he knows that you cannot turn back the clock. We are reminded that the noble phrases of the Declaration of Independence are a standard that the United States must always measure itself against, but one so perfect that no nation could ever hope to live up to it.

● **Activity 4**

Analyse this article to find the phrases the writer uses:
1) to say what happens in the novel;
2) to describe Gatsby and give him greater significance;
3) to connect him with the theme of the United States as a nation.

● **Composition**

1 Describe any important character in the novel or play you are reading in terms of physical and mental characteristics.
2 How do the main characters in the book you are reading contribute to our understanding of the main theme?
3 Describe the hero, heroine or villain in the book in terms of his or her attraction for the reader, using one of the techniques suggested on page 105.

Description: Events

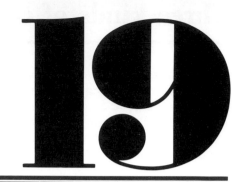

Checklist

● **Sequence of tenses**

Past Simple and Past Perfect, Past Simple and Conditional

I **was** only eight years old when the Second World War **ended**. We **had not suffered** much in the small town where I lived. (The suffering refers to a period previous to the first sentence, 'during the War'.)
Before the War, things **had been** better; when the War **was** over, we **would go back** to London. (Thinking back and forward in time from a time in the past.)

Present, Future and Conditional

By the year 2050 scientists **estimate** that man **will be able** to construct permanent settlements. The first islands **would be** energy stations.

(We use **will** in the first sentence because, according to our present knowledge, we will be able to achieve the building of permanent settlements. When we start talking about these settlements, as in the second sentence, we use **would** because we are referring to a hypothetical situation.)

● **Can and could (Conditional)**

Unless the settlers **can find** a way of growing plants, the atmosphere **will not be maintained**. But if the 'planet' **could spin** round, plants **could be grown** and the inhabitants **would have** a feeling of stability. (The second sentence is still a hypothesis.)

● **Such as and like**

There are no bullfights here, **such as** you might see in the south.
There are no bullfights here, **like** those (the ones) you might see in the south.

(**Like** can only be used for comparison, followed by a noun or pronoun.)

● **Both, also, too, as well**

Both at home **and** at school I had become accustomed to these phrases.
At home **and also** at school I had become accustomed to these phrases.
I had become accustomed to these phrases at home **and** at school, **too. (as well)**

● **Specially and especially**

The other dances take place in early summer, **especially** at Whitsun.
The Space Shuttle, has the enormous advantage of being **specially designed** to return to Earth.

(**Especially** is the correct form, unless the word is followed by a past participle, such as **made, built, designed**.)

● **Reflexive verbs**

I **let myself** in with the front-door key.

Study Reference Section — Reflexive verbs, page 159.
See Book 3, Exercises 19A—D.

19.1 Three kinds of composition

The passages that follow in this unit describe, respectively, a historical event in the past, seen from the point of view of personal experience (the opposite page); events that happen regularly, such as festivals or annual holidays, (pages 110–11); and possible events in the future (page 12). Any of these topics may be set in the First Certificate examination. The advice provided here is meant to show you what differences are involved in writing such compositions, not only in grammatical terms but also in terms of planning. If you are in doubt, refer back to this page when you are doing the activities in the unit or writing one of the compositions at the end of this unit.

Past events

The passage on the opposite page is similar to a narrative, with one important exception. It is necessary to explain the historical background to the event for people who may not know very much about it. However, if you want to attract the reader's attention, you will probably begin by mentioning the event and then refer back to the background. See the table below for tenses.

Recurring events

Events that happen regularly may not be happening at this moment. The main descriptive tense will be the Present Simple, not the Present Continuous. The Past tenses, for narrative, will only be used if you mention a particular occasion in the past when, for example, something unusual happened.

Remember that you are not describing a single historic event or one that is historic (i.e. that has become famous in history). Instead of giving the historical background, you may have to explain the origin of a custom or a ceremony.

Future events

Bear in mind that in this case we have no personal experience of what is going to happen in the future. Consequently we cannot use the Future with **will** as the main tense throughout except in Conditional sentences. (If A happens, B will happen). In most cases, what we think about the future is hypothesis. Before you attempt to do such compositions yourself, study the passage on page 112, and notice how the sentences with **will** are replaced by sentences using **would**.

	PAST	PRESENT	FUTURE
Main tense	Past Simple	Present Simple	**If/When** … + Future with **will**
Secondary tense	Past Perfect Simple	Past Simple	Conditional (**would**)
PLAN	1 Event 2 Historical background 3 What happened 4 Conclusion: Historical importance	1 Event 2 Origin of custom, etc. 3 What usually happens 4 Why event is still popular; its significance	1 Relationship to present 2 Predictions for the future 3 Hypothesis based on predictions 4 What the future will be like if predictions and hypothesis are true

● VE Day, May 8th, 1945

I was only eight years old when the Second World War ended, but I can still remember something about the victory celebrations in the small town where I lived on the day when the war in Europe ended. We had not suffered much from the war there, though, like most children of my age, I was used to seeing bombed houses in the streets and the enormous army lorries passing through. But both at home and at school I had become accustomed to the phrases 'before the war' and 'when the war's over'. 'Before the war', apparently, things had been better, though I was too young to understand why, except that there had been no bombs then, and people had eaten things like ice cream and bananas, which I had only heard of. When the war was over we would go back to London, but this meant very little to me. I did not remember what London was like.

What I remember now about VE Day was the afternoon and the evening. I remember coming home about five o'clock with a little girl of my age who lived in the house opposite. Some boys and girls on a bomb-site at the end of the street were collecting wood and building an enormous bonfire. We stood and watched them for a time, and then I went home and let myself in with my key and waited for my parents to come back from work.

It was May and still broad daylight when my mother arrived, and my father came in about an hour later. After dinner I said I wanted to see the bonfire, so when it got dark my father took me to the end of the street. The bonfire was very high, and somehow people had collected some old clothes to dress the unmistakable figure with the moustache they had put on top of it. Just as we arrived, they set light to it. The flames rose and soon engulfed the 'guy'. Everyone was cheering and shouting, and an old woman came out of her house with two chairs and threw them on the fire to keep the blaze going.

I stood beside my father until the fire started to go down, not knowing what to say. He said nothing, either. He had fought in the First World War and may have been remembering the end of that. At last he said, 'Well, that's it, son. Let's hope that this time it really will be the last one'.

● Activity 1

1 This story is told almost in chronological order, but with one important exception. Find the exception, and consider whether the story would be so easy to understand if the order had been completely chronological.

2 Why is the last paragraph separated from the one before? Is there a change of emphasis? Why is direct speech used?

3 Plan a description of an important historical event you have been involved in or have seen on television.

19.3 Recurring events

● **Festivals**

People still celebrate ancient festivals in different parts of Europe with folk dances and processions, even though in many cases those who take part and put on special costumes are no longer sure what the dances represent. Almost all of them are associated with seasonal rituals that have been adapted to the Christian calendar. There are two main types found in a number of countries. The first, combat dances, normally take place in winter or early spring and celebrate the battle between the old year and the new. In Austria, for example, at carnival time, people wear masks and dress up as ghosts and witches, and there are processions of men and women with drums and whips. In Spain the battle has been transformed into one between Christians and Moors. A friend of mine, who comes from a village near Alicante on the Mediterranean coast, goes home every year to take part in the festival, which lasts three days. He has to dress up as a Moor because his family have always played that part, and the costumes are passed from one generation to the next. The festival is carefully planned, so he knows that his side will win on the second day, but lose on the first and third.

The other main group of dances takes place in early summer, especially at Whitsun or on May Day. In England, there are dances of morris men in some villages. Groups of trained dancers, dressed in white, dance with bells on their legs and bodies. They leap in processions in double files, waving white handkerchiefs or green branches. In some places, there are men with animal masks or a Jack-in-the-Green, a man dressed in leaves who stands for the new vegetation of the summer.

● **Activity 2**

Discuss any ceremony you are familiar with, such as a marriage or christening, or a folk dance or festival where people dress up in special clothes. Make notes on their dress and actions so that you can explain what happens to other members of the class.

Question: Describe a typical annual celebration in your country.

Subject: A village <u>fiesta</u> in Spain

Plan: 1) The meaning of the celebration, when it is held.

2) What happens during the day.

3) What happens in the evening.

Details: Costumes worn, differences from other countries or regions.

Emphasis: Personal experience.

Every Spanish village has a special day once a year as a holiday. This is called the <u>fiesta mayor</u>. Because of the different origins of the people who live in different parts of the country, however, it is not celebrated in the same way everywhere. In my village in Catalonia, for example, there are no bullfights or religious processions such as you might see in the south.

In the morning, the majority of people get up late, except for those who go to Mass, and the children, who go to play in the main square, where there are swings and roundabouts and other sideshows to amuse them. Before lunch most people go for a walk towards the centre of the village to greet their friends and listen to the band playing <u>sardanas</u> (the <u>sardana</u> is the Catalan national dance). The band are dressed in the national costume, with red caps, white shirts and black trousers, and a few of the men who come to watch wear this costume, too. Sometimes there is a football match against a team from a neighbouring village, but in my village this is played in the afternoon, because our <u>fiesta mayor</u> is in July and it is too hot to play at midday. All the men and boys go to the match and the referee has to do his best to help the home side to win. This is not quite fair, but everyone knows that when it is the other village's <u>fiesta</u>, it will be their turn.

In the evening, there is a kind of party in the main square, with sandwiches and hot seusages and sweets, all provided by the village. Afterwards, when it gets dark, everyone sits round waiting for the dance to begin. These days, there is usually a popular singer for the young people, and after that the <u>sardanas</u>. The <u>sardana</u> is a wonderfully friendly dance, because everyone joins hands to form big groups. About one o'clock in the morning, when the children are tired, people begin to go home, but some go on dancing and celebrating in the two village bars till the early hours of the morning.

MOVING HOUSE
INTO SPACE?

The first flight of the Space Shuttle Columbia in the spring of 1981 was a revolutionary development in space exploration. Unlike the rockets of the previous twenty years, Columbia has the enormous advantage of being specially designed to return to Earth and make further flights. Among the large number of projects scientists are investigating for its future use, the most exciting, perhaps, is that the first steps can now be taken towards establishing human colonies in space. The present Space Shuttle can only stay in space for about a week, but it could take people out to build 'islands' where they could stay for longer periods. By the year 2050 scientists estimate that man will be able to construct permanent settlements.

The first 'islands' would be energy stations. There would be no hope of establishing colonies in space unless people could obtain energy there, instead of getting it from Earth. However, if the original settlers could convert solar energy into electricity, it would be possible to provide the equivalent of a filling station for cars on Earth, allowing the Space Shuttle to refuel and stay in orbit for longer periods of time.

If this initial project were

successful, much larger solar energy stations would be constructed with materials brought out by the Shuttle. There would be enough food and water for astronauts to stay there for three months. Bases like this would be built fairly near the Earth, but astronauts could use them to assemble craft that would take them much further out. It would still be optimistic to think of exploring planets, however. The Shuttle, at its present speed, would take over two months to reach Venus, the nearest planet.

Eventually man would be able to construct an inhabitable 'planet' in space. It would have to be airtight, because settlers would not want to spend all their time in space suits. It would be quite small and unless the settlers could find a way of growing plants, the atmosphere would not be maintained. But if the 'planet' could spin round, so that everything was held to the walls by a kind of gravity, plants could be grown and the inhabitants would have a feeling of stability. What would they do there? At first, they would probably be mainly concerned with staying alive, but almost certainly, if all these technological advances ever come about, man will have the ingenuity to find things for them to do.

● **Activity 3**

Make a list of the things that you think people will be able to do by the year 2000 that we cannot do now. If we could do these things, what changes would take place in the world?

● **Composition**

1 Describe a folk dance or festival in your country, or a wedding you have attended.
2 Describe an important event you have witnessed in real life or on television.
3 Describe the changes you expect to find in your town in the year 2000. What do you think it will be like?

Complaining and apologising

Checklist

● **Conditional sentences (4)**

See also Unit 17.

If you**'d (had) told** me, I**'d** (**would**) **have helped** you.

If you**'d arrived** on time, you **wouldn't have missed** the beginning of the film.

Note the use of **might have** and **could have**:

If he **hadn't braked** sharply, he **might have knocked** the old lady **down**. (= perhaps he would have ...)

It's such a pity I didn't see you, because there were so many things we **could have done** together (if we **had met**). (= we would have been able to do if we had met.)

See Book 3, Exercise 57.

● **Why (not) and should (shouldn't) have**

Should have and **shouldn't have** with the past participle automatically suggest that the person didn't do what was right or did something that was wrong.

Why didn't you tell me you were going to be late?

You should have told me you were going to be late.

Why did you throw those books **away**? I needed them.

You shouldn't have thrown those books **away**. I needed them.

Study Reference Section — Modals, page 149.

● **Perfect infinitive**

I'm sorry **to have kept** you waiting. (You were waiting.)

I'm sorry **to have kept** you waiting. (You were waiting until now.)

● **Shall we and let's**

Both are invitations, but the first is a question, the second a much stronger form, urging the other person to do something with the speaker.

Shall we go in? I think the film's going to start soon.

Let's go in. The film's going to start soon.

Study Reference Section — Modals, page 149.

● **Polite suggestions/invitations/requests**

I **was wondering** if you**'d be** free on Saturday.

If you **were**, we **could go** out.

Compare:

If you**'re** free on Saturday, we **can go** out. (A straightforward condition, implying that the other person will accept.)

20.1 Informal complaint and apology

● **Dialogue 1** 📼

Listen to the dialogue.

MUM Tammie, what have you done?

TAMMIE I'm sorry, Mum. I was trying to cook a rice dish for supper from this recipe, but I put too much water in the rice and it boiled over.

MUM Just look at the cooker! And it's gone all over the floor, too.

TAMMIE Sorry, Mum. I was just going to clean it up. If you'd arrived in five minutes' time, you wouldn't have noticed it.

MUM Why didn't you tell me you were doing rice? If you'd told me, I'd have come and helped you.

TAMMIE Well, I would have called you, but I wanted it to be a surprise.

● **Activity 1 — pair work**

Make up a dialogue for one of these situations:
1 a cake that got burnt;
2 some plates that got broken during the washing-up;
3 a soup that was spoilt because someone put sugar in it instead of salt.
One speaker should complain and the other should apologise and explain what happened.

● **Dialogue 2** 📼

Listen to the dialogue.

PAM Where on earth have you been, Colin? I've been waiting here half an hour. The main film's already started.

COLIN I'm sorry to have kept you waiting, love, honestly, but I really couldn't help it. You see...

PAM They kept you late at the office again.

COLIN Well, yes, that's right. I just couldn't get away.

PAM From your friends in the Swan!

COLIN No, of course not. But then the car wouldn't start, you see...

PAM Well, you should have phoned the cinema and left a message. I've been standing outside in this freezing cold wind for half an hour!

COLIN Well, you needn't have done that. I mean, you could have gone inside and had a drink.

PAM Or I could have caught a bus and met you at the Swan, I suppose!

COLIN No, well, that wouldn't have been any good, would it? I mean, I wasn't there. I've just explained all that to you. But I really am sorry, darling. It won't happen again, I promise.

PAM It had better not! Well, let's go in. I'm freezing.

● **Activity 2 — pair work**

Make up a dialogue between:
1 a man who is late to meet his girlfriend;
2 a girl who is late to meet her boyfriend;
3 a friend who is late for an appointment with another.

Aristofanus 99
Kifisa
Athens
Greece

12 March, 1984

Dear Sue

I only received your letter yesterday when I got back from holiday.
I was terribly sorry to have missed you, because there were so many
things we could have done and talked about, and of course I would
have loved to take you round the city.

If I had known you were coming I would have come back earlier.
I wasn't far away, in fact. We were staying for a few days with
some relatives of ours in Nauplion, because my father's health
hasn't been too good recently and the doctor told him he should
get away from work for a while. So I took time off work - in fact
I only had two weeks off from the shop last summer and I still
had two weeks' holiday to come - and the rest has done me a lot of
good too.

What a pity we couldn't meet! Anyway, I hope you all had a lovely
time. They say that once you drink the water of Athens you'll always
come back, so I hope we shall see you here before long. What about
this summer?

Regards to your family.

Love

Efi

Efi.

---

27 Castle Mount
Hathersage
Derbyshire
England

1 March 1984

Dear Sofia

I'm sorry this is such short notice - if I'd known about it before
I would have written to you earlier - but I'm coming out to Greece
for a few days' holiday with my parents and we shall be in Athens
next weekend. They're really coming to have a rest in the sun. If

But I was wondering if you'd be free on Saturday or Sunday. If
you were, the two of us could meet and you could show me some
of your fascinating city.

Again, I'm sorry for not having let you know earlier. I told
my parents they should have made up their minds about the holiday
months ago, but you know what they're like! And I can't really
complain because they've invited me. Needless to say, everybody
at work envies me like mad!

You can't imagine how much I'm looking foward to my first visit to
Greece. According to the weather chart in the papers, you're
having what we would consider summer weather. Here it's grim,
and believe it or not we've got snow on the hills around us.

Looking foward very much to seeing you.

Regards to your family,

Love

Sue

Sue

REASON
R WRITING

SUCCESTION

APOLOGY

FRIENDLY
ENDING

ENDING

● **Activity 3 — pair/group work**

1 Read the two letters above. Plan a letter to
a friend in another country, informing
him/her of a visit you are going to make to
his/her town. Plan a reply in which your
friend writes, saying that unfortunately
he/she will not be there.

2 Plan a letter from a friend telling you that
he/she is coming to your town. You will not
be there, but write immediately, saying what
you could do together if the dates could be
changed.

20.2 Formal complaint and apology

16 Coronation Avenue
Chatham Gate

The Manager
Customer Services Dept
National Railway Company   17 December 1983
11 Fleet Street
Bogshead

Dear Sir

REASON FOR
COMPLAINT

In company with many other commuters, I have to use the surburban
train service between Chatham Gate and Bogshead Central every working
day. I say 'have to' because for a long time the service has been
unreliable, unpunctual and uncomfortable, but we regular travellers
have been putting up with these faults because there is no alternative
means of public transport into Bogshead.

SPECIFIC
EXAMPLES

However, there are limits to a traveller's patience, even on the
Chatham Gate-Bogshead line, and I think many of us passed well beyond
those limits last night on the so-called 6.19 train from Bogshead
Central. To begin with, the train left Bogshead at 6.27, already
8 minutes late, and arrived in Bogshead Junction at 6.37, after an
unscheduled stop of five minutes at a signal. In Bogshead Junction
we stood for 30 minutes, instead of the scheduled two, and, as no
information to explain the delay was given at any time, we began to
think the company had simply forgotten the train was there. To cut
a long story short, we finally arrived in Chatham Gate, after two
more stops at signals on the way, at 7.50 - 30 minutes late.

The delay would have been more bearable if the train had had it's
usual six carriages. In fact, since there were a lot of Christmas
shoppers on the train as well as we poor regular travellers, even if
the train had had six carriages last night it would have been
overcrowded. But last night, for the first time in the six years I
have been using the train, there were only three, and we were packed
together like sardines.

It would be interesting to see how the National Railway Company explains
this sort of inefficiency, which is all too common. If the company had
only taken the trouble to explain and apologise for the delay last night,
I would not have felt the need to write this letter.

Yours truly

Helen Stopford

Helen Stopford

NATIONAL RAILWAY COMPANY

Mrs H Stopford
16 Coronation Avenue
Chatham Gate

20 December 1983

Dear Mrs Stopford

On behalf of NRC Eastern Region, I should like to apologise for the inconvenience to you and all the passengers on the 6.19 train from Bogshead to Chatham Gate on Friday December 16, and to take the opportunity of explaining why, in recent weeks, the standard of our surburban services has not been as high as usual.

To begin with, I should like to mention that since the beginning of November, the flu epidemic which is affecting the whole area has hit the company very hard, and if it had not been for the chronic staffing problem it has caused, I'm sure the trouble on the 6.19 (and on many other trains where there have been unavoidable delays) would not have happened.

We trust that there will soon be an end to the flu epidemic and that before long we shall be able to provide our normal services. I would like to reassure you and the public in general that, in the meantime, we shall do our best to reduce inconvenience to a minimum.

Yours sincerely

Peter Parkinson

Peter Parkinson
Public Relations Manager, National Railway Company (Eastern Region)

National Railway Company (Eastern Region), 11 Fleet Street, Bogshead

● **Activity 4**

1 Read the letter of complaint on page 116 and list all the writer's specific complaints.
2 Read the letter of apology above. Find the specific complaints from the first letter that the manager replies to and tick them on your list.
3 From your list, find those complaints which do not receive an adequate reply in the manager's letter and say what he **should have said**.

Giovanna Fanfani, an Italian student, went to London as a tourist in the first two weeks of March, 1984, and while she was there she bought a Sony XR2 music centre at the Alick Smart Hi-Fi Shop. At the same time she wanted to buy replacement styluses, but didn't for the reasons that become clear from the following letter, which is the shop manager's *reply* to Giovanna's letter of complaint.

Alick Smart Hi-Fi
Burke Street
London W13
England

Ms G Fanfani
Via Manzoni 138
20121 Milan
<u>Italy</u>

27 March 1984

Dear Ms Fanfani

Thank you for your letter, which we received today. We are sorry that one of our assistants gave you the wrong information, and you are quite right that he should have known which models Sony markets in Italy; but we would ask you to bear in mind that there are now so many different models that we find it very difficult to keep up to date with such information.

However, we have pleasure in informing you that we have a good stock of DD2 diamond styluses, at a cost per unit of £9.95. Postage and packing for six of these would amount to £2.45, so your International Money Order should be made out to the value of £62.15. As soon as we receive your confirmation of the order and the I.M.O. we shall despatch the goods.

We hope that your XR2 Music Centre will give you lots of excellent listening, and that you will visit us again when you are next in London.

Yours sincerely

Jim Lenska

Jim Lenska
<u>Manager</u>

● **Activity 5 — pair work**

Read the manager's letter and then plan and write the letter you think Giovanna wrote to the shop. Your letter will need three sections: 1) reason for writing; 2) cause of complaint; 3) suggested solution.

● **Composition**

1 You have been corresponding with a penfriend for five years, but you live very far apart and you have never had the chance to meet. Write a letter in which you suggest a meeting.
2 You recently made a flight with Transoceanic Airlines in which your luggage was lost (temporarily), there was a mistake in the booking of your ticket, and you were kept waiting seven hours before the departure without any information. Write a letter of complaint to Transoceanic.
3 You went on a package holiday to London and stayed in a hotel where the door of your room had a faulty lock. You discover when you arrive home that something you bought has been lost, and you're sure you had it in the hotel. Write to the hotel to complain.

Discussion: Choosing an approach

Checklist

● **Conditionals without if clause**

I **would favour** a shorter working week, but I **would provide** more entertainment facilities. This in turn **would provide** more employment.

(The writer is forming a hypothesis of what **would happen** if he or she had the power to change the present situation.)

● **Emphatic forms**

... our teenage children. They suffer most. They are **the ones who** suffer most. **It's they** (our children) **who/that** suffer most. (Stronger forms of **They suffer most**.)

Personally, I have no objection. Susan doesn't agree. Susan is **the one** (person) **who** doesn't agree. **It's Susan who/that** doesn't agree. (Stronger forms of **Susan doesn't agree**.)

Do emphasises the repetition of the verb already used.

He said you didn't like apples. — But I **do** like them.

Smoking goes on all the time in drama series, where it's used as a sign of anxiety. — But in real life people **do** smoke because they're anxious.

● **Clauses of concession (2) — in spite of, although**

In spite of the improvements in working conditions (**in spite of** working conditions **having improved**), the average working week is still over 40 hours in most European countries. (**In spite of** + noun/gerund) **Although** working conditions **have improved**, the average working week is still over 40 hours... (**Although** + finite verb)

See Book 3, Exercise 59.

● **Fewer and less**

Fewer is used with count nouns, **less** with non-count nouns.

Workers would like to get paid the same for **fewer hours** of work, but employers are convinced that **less work** would be done and that they would make **less profit**.

See Book 3, Exercises 20A—B.

21.1 Recognising a standpoint

● **Activity 1**

Three speakers are discussing the topic of smoking on television on a radio programme; they are Allan Piper of the MacAdam Tobacco Co., Dr Marion Stark, a psychologist, and Laura Franklin, who belongs to a group campaigning against smoking. Read the transcript of the discussion. Imagine what sort of person is likely to have the views expressed. Then fit the speeches to the characters.

When you have done this, listen to the dialogue.

● **Dialogue**

1 In the first place I'd like to make it clear that we realise it would be impossible to ban smoking from TV entirely. For instance, we could hardly cut Humphrey Bogart's cigarettes out of his mouth! What we are aiming at is to reduce smoking being shown unnecessarily in plays, interviews, chat shows and so on.

2 There's an obvious question here that everyone in my — that is, the tobacco — industry would like a clear answer to, and that is: What do you hope to achieve by banning smoking?

3 Well, naturally, we hope more and more people will give up smoking as a result and that fewer and fewer will start. TV is a very powerful medium, and people should be protected against that power, because it's strong enough to persuade them to do things to themselves that cause them lasting harm.

4 So what you really want to do is to protect the public from its own — what shall we say — weakness, stupidity...?

5 Well, that's hardly the way I'd put it. What I'd say would be...

6 That's hardly fair, is it, Allan? Young people, for example, especially young teenagers, are not fully aware of the risks.

7 But it is the basis of Ms Franklin's argument, surely. Her organisation believes, fundamentally, that people, most people at least, are just not intelligent enough, or not mature enough, to make up their own minds.

8 Hm. That, of course, is the sort of argument I'd expect from someone in the tobacco industry. You'd like to make out that anyone who campaigns against smoking is some kind of fanatic determined to take away people's freedom of choice, and pose as the defender of liberty. But you know as well as I do that that's not the point at issue here. You know how powerful TV is, more powerful than most people realise, and it's precisely because they don't realise it, that it's so dangerous.

9 But cigarette advertisements have been banned for years on TV!

10 And quite right, too, but that isn't our main object now. What we want to do now is to attack the habit of smoking itself. Smoking goes on all the time in drama series, for instance, where it's used as a sign of sophistication, or inner tension, or toughness, or anxiety. Now I'm sure you're not going to tell me that professional actors can't convey these feelings without cigarettes.

11 But drama is supposed to reflect real life, isn't it? In real life people do smoke because they're anxious.

12 Could I interrupt for a moment to clarify one or two points? First, what Laura is saying, or rather implying, is that TV can be used to change social habits, people's behaviour, and so on. So, just as TV may make an association in viewers' minds between smoking and relaxation, it could also — if styles of acting were changed — it could also be used to break that association and replace it with a different one. For instance, actors could express anxiety by drumming their fingers on the table, and then people would stop associating cigarettes with relief from anxiety. Secondly...

13 Exactly. Association is very important. Fifty years ago people didn't associate relaxation with smoking...

14 Do you mind if I come in on that point?

15 Just a moment, please. I hadn't quite finished. Secondly, though the power of association is quite clear, people are not going to stop being anxious because smoking disappears from TV. In fact, this raises the point that you may be doing them harm psychologically if you persuade them, directly or indirectly, to give up smoking without offering them an adequate alternative way to relax...

● **Activity 2 — group work**

1 Choose one of the topics below. List all the points that could be made for and against each statement. Decide which would be emphasised by: a) someone in favour; b) someone against; c) someone who sees both sides and is undecided.
   1 All uses of nuclear power should be banned.
   2 There should be a tax on sweets to protect public health.
   3 There should be no censorship of any kind.
2 Each person should prepare a talk lasting two or three minutes on a topic he/she feels strongly about. The others can intervene during the talk with comments or questions. Give the talk from notes. Don't write it out as a speech.

● **Activity 3 — Balloon debate**

Four or five famous people are in a balloon. They will only be saved if one is thrown overboard. Choose the part of a famous person and give a short talk to explain why you should be saved, rather than the others. Then vote to decide who should be thrown overboard.

21.2 Choosing *your* approach

A composition in which you are asked to give your opinion is best answered by one of three approaches: 1) you have strong views for or against the proposition and want to convince other people; 2) you do not feel strongly but can see points on both sides; 3) you may feel in favour of the proposition or against it in general terms but your opinion is that it presents or depends on other problems.

Read these three compositions and decide which is 1), which is 2) and which is 3). Note the approach in each case: 1) states a point of view clearly, answers opposing arguments and makes a suggestion for resolving difficulties; 2) is balanced, showing the points for and against alternately, without taking sides. The solution is a possible third way out; 3) considers the kind of person who is for or against such a proposition, asks questions about it and raises what the writer thinks is the real problem involved, giving a solution. Find evidence for these points in the compositions.

A

Question: 'The normal working week should be 30 hours.' Do you agree?

If the idea of working only 30 hours a week appeals to you, it is probably because you do not like your work and you imagine that you could spend the extra hours enjoying yourself. Those whose jobs interest them, on the other hand, reject the idea. They know that the hours of work you do officially are not the main factor in the argument, because some people work more intensively than others, and the ones that work hardest think about their jobs when they are at home.

The advantages of a shorter working week are in any case not as clear as they may appear. Would the week mean fewer hours every day or, for example, not working on Fridays? I once worked in a firm where we had to vote on a choice like this. All the men voted to go home half an hour earlier every day, and all the women preferred to have Friday afternoon off to do the shopping for the weekend.

The real problem here is that work is unpleasant and boring for a lot of people, but they have not developed enough interests to keep them occupied away from the office or the factory. Now that a lot of young people are unemployed you often see them spending all morning in an amusement arcade, wasting their time and money on machines. It would cost a lot of money to reduce the working week to 30 hours.

I would rather spend it on creating more interesting jobs and educating people in their working hours so that they would enjoy their spare time more.

Question: 'The normal working week should be 30 hours.' Do you agree?

It is extraordinary that in spite of the improvements in working conditions in this century, the average working week is still over 40 hours in most European countries, and on top of that a large number of workers do several hours' overtime. This seems ridiculous when unemployment is so high. If the working week were only 30 hours, everyone would have more spare time and most of the unemployed people could find work.

Of course those who do oppose a reduction in the working week argue that people would not know what to do with their leisure, and anyway the country could not afford it, because we are continually being told to work harder. Yet the main reason why people do not work hard enough is because they are tired, and the main reason why they do overtime is because they earn more money during those extra working hours, so they prefer to work slowly so that overtime will be necessary.

I would certainly favour a shorter working week to give people time to pursue their own interests, but I would provide more entertainment facilities and educational courses for them to develop these interests. This in turn would provide more employment. The main argument against a 30-hour week is that companies could not afford it, but if there were no unemployment and everyone went to work feeling fresh and relaxed, they would do as much as they do now and would not be worried by the fear of losing their jobs.

C

Question: 'The normal working week should be 30 hours.' Do you agree?

At first it seems a good idea that people should only have to work 30 hours a week. Those in favour argue that workers deserve more spare time to enjoy their private interests. Of course, they assume that the workers would earn the same amount of money; otherwise, they would not be able to afford their leisure activities.

On the other hand, many people argue that we depend on work to fill up our lives. They are afraid that if we had a lot more time with nothing to do we would not know how to use it. They say ordinary people often lack imagination to amuse themselves, so they would be bored and spend all day watching television.

Workers would no doubt like to get paid the same for fewer hours of work, employers, however, are convinced that less work would be done so they would have to employ more people and make less profit. Again, there are two sides to the question, because workers would probably work harder if they did not have to work such long hours; on the other hand, it would not be easy to persuade them to do as much in 30 hours as they did in 40.

Personally, I think the solution lies in making jobs more interesting or in giving workers longer holidays or opportunities to study during working hours; in that way, they would not waste their spare time.

● **Activity 4**

Choose a topic from the list below and decide on your approach. Plan the approach, making short notes for a two-minute speech to the class.

1 Taxation should be reduced.
2 War toys should be banned.
3 Children should be taught a foreign language at primary school.
4 Private cars should not be allowed in town centres.
5 People should not be allowed to keep animals as pets in the city.

21.3 Tracing an argument

● **Activity 5**

The first paragraph of the article below is the only one printed in the correct position. Reorder the other paragraphs, giving reasons for your choice. Then look back to pages 122−3 and decide which of the three types of approach the writer of this article is using.

Television censorship

1 A lot of people believe that television has a harmful effect on children. Thirty or forty years ago, the same criticisms were made of the cinema. But although child psychologists have spent a great deal of time studying this problem, there is not much evidence that television brings about juvenile delinquency.

2 This volume of correspondence clearly indicates that parents are concerned about what their children see. It is therefore surprising that, while they complain about programmes that deal realistically with many features of modern life, they see no harm in cartoon films for children in which the villain, in some cases a human being, suffers one brutal punishment after another. Apparently, any amount of violence is permissible, providing the background is sufficiently unreal. I doubt whether psychologists would agree with parents that it is harmless.

3 The truth is that different things disturb different children, and parents themselves are likely to react differently on various subjects. Since no one has proved satisfactorily that there is a direct connection between certain films and juvenile delinquency, it is difficult to know where censorship should begin. The only satisfactory solution would seem to be for TV companies to inform viewers about the content of programmes and say whether they think they are suitable for children. It would then be the parents' responsibility, as it should be in any case, to decide whether their categories coincide with the TV companies', and whether children should see them.

4 Parents have always exercised censorship on behalf of their children, but it has not always been of the same kind. A hundred years ago, writers for children carefully avoided any reference to sex in their books but had no inhibitions about including scenes of violence. These days children are often brought up to think freely about sex, but violence is discouraged. Nevertheless, television companies receive a large number of letters every week complaining about programmes with adult themes being shown at times when a few young children may be awake.

5 Perhaps the most surprising thing of all, since the protests often concern programmes shown late in the evening, is that the children are not already in bed. Another remarkable thing is that if the parents find programmes objectionable, they do not turn off the television. One cannot help thinking that parents of this kind want to thrust their own responsibilities onto the TV companies because they are too selfish or lazy to censor programmes themselves.

● **Composition**

Write about one of the topics from Activity 2 or Activity 4 of this Unit.

Wishes, regrets and complaints

Checklist

● Wish and if only

Wishes

Wishes are expressed in the Past tense when they refer to the present or future.

I wish (If only) **I was (were)** old enough to leave school.
If I **was (were)** old enough, I**'d get** a job and earn some money.
I wish (If only) we **lived** by the sea.
If we **lived** by the sea, we **could buy** a boat and I **could go** fishing.

Regrets

Wishes referring to the past are regrets, because the opportunity no longer exists. They are expressed in the Past Perfect tense.

I wish (If only) I**'d had** the chance of going to university.
If I**'d had** the chance, I **wouldn't have had to** take the first job that came along.

Complaints

I wish (and sometimes **if only**) is used with the Conditional (**would**) to express a complaint to or about someone. It refers to present time or time in general — what people always do.

I wish you**'d be** more careful with your things (= Why aren't you...?)
I wish he **wouldn't drop** his cigarette ash on the carpet (= Why does he...?)

See Book 3, Exercises 60A—B, 98B.

● Co-ordinating relative clauses

I've just spent the weekend with Uncle Harold, **which** ought to qualify me for some kind of medal. (**Which** refers to the whole of the previous clause, not to Uncle Harold.)

Study Reference Section — Relative clauses, page 157.
See Book 3, Exercise 62.

● As, like and as if

As if is followed by the Past tense if the comparison is untrue, or unreal.

He treated me **as** a human being. (I am a human being.)
They treated me **like** a king. (I am not a king.)
It looks **as if** we**'ll have to** visit the rig tomorrow. (= We'll probably have to visit it.)
It's **as if** they **wanted** to keep us here. (But they don't.)

22.1 In conversation

● Dialogues 1–4

Listen to these four short dialogues.

Dialogue 1

COLIN I hate asking my Dad for money. If only I was old enough to leave school. Then I'd get a job and earn some money, and I wouldn't have to rely on him all the time.

DAVID I know how you feel. But you wouldn't get a very good job if you left school at sixteen, would you? And you probably wouldn't earn much, either.

Dialogue 2

ELSIE I wish we lived by the sea, Dad. Then I could go swimming every day.

FATHER Yes, it would be nice, wouldn't it? We could buy a boat and I could go fishing.

Dialogue 3

GERRY I wish we could see each other every evening. If only we didn't have all these exams to worry about.

JILL I know. I wish we had more time together, too.

GERRY If only it was July already, and we were lying on the beach on holiday!

JILL Hmm, cheer up, though. It's not too long to wait.

Dialogue 4

INGRID If only I could sing like Sue! She's got a wonderful voice.

JASON Yes. I wish I could play the guitar like Cliff, too. I could accompany you. If we got really good at it, we could form a group.

INGRID Yes, it would be great, wouldn't it?

● Activity 1 — pair work

Think of several things that you have always wanted to be/do/have, or circumstances that you would like to be different. Tell your partner about your daydreams.
Say: **I wish (If only) I had..., I wish (If only) I lived..., I wish I could..., I wish I didn't have to...**, etc.
Your partner must comment: **If you..., I wish I ..., too, Yes, that would be ...**, etc.

Listen to these two dialogues.

Dialogue 5

KEITH I wish I'd had the chance of going to university. If I hadn't left school at fourteen, I wouldn't have had to take the first job that came along.

LAURA It's no use worrying about it now, dear. They were difficult times. If things had been different and your father hadn't been out of work, you could have stayed on, but you've done very well, all the same.

KEITH I know. I've no regrets, love. I just wish I could have had more time with you and the kids when we were younger, that's all.

Dialogue 6

MARK God, I'm a fool, Nora! Look at this scratch on the record. If only I'd insisted on seeing it before I left the shop! I should have kept the receipt, too, but I was in such a hurry that I came out without it. I wish I'd never bought the record now.

NORA Don't worry. I'm sure they'll take it back. We've bought a lot of records there. It would be different if they didn't know you.

● Activity 2 — pair work

Is there anything you regret in your life or anything you have done recently that you are sorry about? What would you have done if things had been different? What should you have done?
Say: **I wish (If only) I had ..., I wish I could have ...**
Your partner must comment: **Still, if you had..., perhaps ... would have ...**

Listen to these two dialogues.

Dialogue 7

OLIVE I wish you'd be more careful with your things, Peter. Why don't you put your toys away when you've finished playing with them? I nearly tripped over this train you left on the floor. If I'd stepped on it, I could have broken my ankle.

PETER Sorry, Mum.

Dialogue 8

RITA Your boss is quite a nice man.

SALLY Mr Ellis? Oh, he's all right, but I wish he wouldn't buzz me at five to five, when I'm getting ready to go home. (*The buzzer sounds.*) Yes, Mr Ellis. You see, Rita. Why does he always do that? I wish he'd organise himself a bit. Then he wouldn't be such a nuisance to everyone else.

● Activity 3 — pair work

Think of any habits people in your family or at work or at school have that irritate you. Tell your partner about them.
Say: **I wish he/she would/wouldn't ..., Why does/doesn't he/she...?**
Your partner could suggest ways to get that person to change his/her habits.

22.2 In writing

Tom Clinton has been in Aberdeen on business for several days, negotiating a contract to supply equipment to an oil rig in the North Sea. He writes to his girlfriend, Carol.

Mr Perks writes to the headmaster of his daughter's school to complain about the teaching.

Highland Hotel
19 Glenmore Avenue
Aberdeen

8th September 1984

Carol darling,

I'm sorry we quarrelled on the 'phone last night. I was going to ring you back this morning but I was almost sure you'd be out. I wish this job was over and I could get the next train back to London, but the negotiations are still going on and it looks as if we'll have to make another visit to the rig tomorrow. If only they'd decide, one way or the other, I wouldn't care whether we got the contract or not.

Of course the contract is important to us. If it weren't, we wouldn't be prepared to go on talking day after day. But that's why I lost my temper last night. I wish I could forget about my work when I'm talking to you, but some of the frustration is bound to come through, I suppose.

I'll try and ring again when I get back from the rig. I hope I'll be able to tell you then when I'll be home...

17 Manchester Street
Bagsley
9th March 1984

Dear Headmaster,

I am sick and tired of my daughter, Shirley, coming home and telling us all the nonsense she hears at school. I wish some of your teachers would do some useful work, such as helping the boys and girls to get through their exams, instead of wasting their time organising discussions about pollution, unemployment, racial discrimination and things of that sort. It's as if they were going to a council meeting, not to school.

If some of these bright young teachers of yours had children of their own, they might think twice before putting ideas into the heads of young people. If only they'd get on with their job and stop encouraging kids to argue with their parents about things they know nothing about, I'd be able to sit down and enjoy my dinner in peace when I come home from work, and so would a lot of other parents, I imagine.

I would like to know what you propose to do about this situation.

Yours faithfully
Sidney Perks
Sidney Perks

● **Activity 4**

Find the places in Tom's letter where he is:
1) complaining about something, and
2) wishing that something were different.

How would you finish the letter, if you were Tom?

● **Activity 5 — group work**

Identify the main complaints in Mr Perks's letter. Think of a good reply to each complaint. Then plan a letter of reply from the headmaster.

Carol Mallory is writing to her married sister, Sheila.

Dear Sheila

I've just spent the weekend with Uncle Harold and Aunt Alice, which ought to qualify me for some kind of medal. I feel absolutely exhausted, both mentally and physically. Neither of us has seen them for years, as you know, and if I'd remembered what they were like or imagined how the children (our dear cousins!) would turn out, I'd never have accepted their invitation. The weekend was a disaster from start to finish, and I wish now that I'd found an excuse not to go, which is what is called being wise after the event!

Uncle Harold is all right in his way, but I wish he'd realise that we're living in the 1980s and wouldn't keep reminding everyone of what they were like as children. First he told me that girls didn't wear trousers when he was young unless they worked in factories. Then he brought out pictures of you and me, when you were nine and I was seven, and said sadly, 'How pretty you were then!', which made me feel about 70 years old!...

● Activity 6

Use the information given below to describe the other members of the family and continue Carol's letter. In each case Carol makes a complaint. Think of an example of such behaviour that might have irritated her and suggest what the effect might have been, as in the paragraph about Uncle Harold.

Aunt Alice has nothing interesting to say, but repeats every detail of her conversations with her neighbours: So she said, '...' and then I said, '...'.

Gerald drives badly, turns round to talk to people in the back of the car and beats time to the music on the car radio. He collected Carol from the station when she arrived.

Mary Anne spends all day eating, drinking and cooking and insists on guests trying everything she has just cooked.

Rupert is keen on fresh air, opens all the windows, it is March, remember, and wants guests to go jogging with him.

Marmaduke, the dog, is enormous and enjoys knocking people down, but the family says he is just playful and they do nothing to help.

Finish the letter in the normal way with regards to Sheila and her husband.

22.3 In retrospect

I suppose we have all asked ourselves at one time or another: 'What would I have been like if I had been born in his situation, or hers? Would I have been any different?' Almost certainly we would have been because, while we have a personality we are born with, it is undoubtedly affected by everything around us from that moment on. Obviously, I would have been different if I had grown up in another country, or even in another town, if I had had brothers and sisters, if my mother and father had separated when I was young, or if one of them had died.

I have few regrets about my life. What interests me more is how far chance has decided my life and how far I have been free to make up my own mind. Childhood is a time when most things are decided by parents and teachers, but all children need a little luck to survive. I could have been killed two or three times. Once in particular, when I was about six, I ran across a road in front of a motorcycle, and the delivery man from the grocer's put his arm out of the window of his van and pulled me to safety. But of course this was not pure chance. If I hadn't been fond of Ken, the grocer's man, I wouldn't have stopped playing in the front garden and run to greet him; if Ken hadn't been used to me, he wouldn't have realised what I was going to do. On the other hand, if he hadn't seen the motor cycle in his mirror, I would probably have been run over, anyway.

When I left university I was offered a job in Brazil. If the salary had been more attractive, I would have accepted the job. Instead, I turned it down and took a job in Spain. But if I had gone to Brazil, I might have stayed there for years. I might have married a Brazilian girl. I doubt if I would have married a Spanish girl, as I did.

Some years later, I applied for a job with a publisher. I had been to several interviews, all disagreeable, where people were rude and unpleasant, and I was getting depressed. Then I met someone who treated me as a human being. When he wrote to me afterwards, saying that the firm could not afford to offer me enough money for me to keep my wife and family, I couldn't resist the urge to write back and thank him for being courteous. He asked me to write a book instead, and now I am a full-time writer. Is that chance?

● **Activity 7 — group work**

Each person should describe in full one of the following:
1) an accident that nearly happened to him/her.
2) a turning point in his/her life.
3) an important meeting.

The description should finish with the words:
If X had/hadn't ..., Y would have/ wouldn't have ...

Examples from the text:

1) If Ken **hadn't caught** him, the motorcycle **would have hit** him.
2) If the salary **had been** more attractive, he **would have accepted** the job.
3) If the publisher **hadn't encouraged** him, he **might not have become** a writer.

● **Composition**

1 If you could have three wishes, what would they be, and what do you think would be the result for you?
2 Think of any important incidents that have made a difference to your life. How would things have been different if they had or had not happened? Have you any regrets about them?

Narrative: Highlighting main events

Checklist

● Past Perfect Simple and Continuous

The verbs in the Past Perfect refer to actions previous to the main verbs in the Past.

Shakespeare's son, Hamnet, **was born** in 1584. Soon afterwards, Shakespeare **left** home. He **became** a well-known actor and dramatist in London. In 1594, Hamnet **died**.

(Chronological order, using Past Simple; no discrimination between events.)
Shakespeare's son, Hamnet, **was born** in 1584, and **died** in 1594. In the meantime, Shakespeare **had left** home and **become** a well-known actor and dramatist in London.

(Contrast between Hamnet's life and his father's. The Past Perfect is used because of the reference back from 1594, in the previous sentence.)

When she **left** home, her family **assumed** that she **had gone** to stay with friends. She **had been working** in London for a fortnight and **had** twice **tried** to ring them before they finally **found out** where she **was**/where she **had gone**.

(**Had been working** refers to a continuous action, **had gone** to a single action, **had tried** to a repeated action.)

See Book 3, Exercise 63.

● By (that time)

When she **rang**, the family **were relieved**. **At that moment** they **were discussing** ways of getting in touch with her.
When she **rang**, the family **were relieved**. **By that time** they **had discussed** various ways of trying to find her.

(In the first sentence, the discussion **was taking place when** she rang; in the second, various discussions **had taken place before** that.)

● It used for emphasis

He **did not begin** to worry **until he saw** the money was missing.
It was not until he saw the money was missing **that he began** to worry.
He **had already decided** to ring the police **when he realised** what had happened.
It was only when he had already decided to ring the police **that he realised** what had happened.

THE DISCOVERY OF TUTANKHAMEN'S TOMB

Howard Carter, the archaeologist who discovered Tutankhamen's tomb, **began** working in Egypt in **1892**. At first he was a draughtsman assisting two other archaeologists, Davis and Maspero, but in **1903** he **was appointed** Archaeological Inspector of Lower and Middle Egypt.

The name of Tutankhamen **was** almost unknown when Davis **found** a few objects referring to him in the Valley of the Kings, near Thebes, in **1906-7**. The contents of the subterranean chamber where he made his finds, however, were badly damaged, and in **1909** Davis **abandoned** the search, saying, 'I fear the Valley of the Kings is now exhausted'.

Meanwhile, in **1907**, a rich aristocrat, Lord Carnarvon, **had arrived** in Egypt and Maspero **had introduced** Carter to him. Lord Carnarvon was impressed by Carter's qualities and from **1908-12** they **explored** the western region of Thebes together, on the left bank of the Nile. When Carnarvon returned to England, he continued to subsidise Carter's work. Maspero, unlike Davis, did not give up hope of finding Tutankhamen's tomb. He believed that it must be in the area explored by Davis.

Nevertheless, in **1912**, Carter **moved** north to dig in the Nile Delta at Sais. That region proved too difficult. No work could be done before April because the land was soaked by the Nile, and when the temperature rose sharply, the diggers were literally chased from the site by cobras. Perhaps because of these snakes, sacred to the ancient Egyptians, Carter **decided** to resume work near Thebes in **1914**.

Although his work was held up by the First World War, Carter **was** eventually **able to make** a systematic exploration of much of the western sector of the Valley of the Kings **from 1919-21** and reach the conclusion that the tomb of Tutankhamen must lie between those of Rameses III and Rameses VI. During **the summer and autumn of 1922**, he **began** to be discouraged, however, and Lord Carnarvon in England began to wonder if any important discovery would ever be made. But on the morning of **November 4th**, digging under Rameses VI's tomb, Carter **saw** what looked like the beginning of a step cut in the rock. It was followed by others that led to a screen of stone plastered over and bearing the seals of a royal burial place. After sixteen steps, a name could be seen: Nebkheprure-Tutankhamen.

Carter informed his patron in England, and a **fortnight later** Lord Carnarvon and his daughter **landed** in Alexandria. They **reached** Luxor, opposite Thebes, on **November 23rd**, and on **the 25th** the first stone **was removed** from the wall of the tomb. Through the small opening, after Carter's first, quick glance, they were able to see strange animals, statues and gold. The sight they saw was the reward for Carter's 30 years of perseverance and hard work and Lord Carnarvon's patient, generous support.

● **Activity 1**

The story on this page is told almost entirely in chronological order in the Past Simple. It is accurate, but does not emphasise the important events enough, mainly because their order in time, not their intrinsic importance, controls the narrative. List what the most important events were before looking at the opposite page.

THE DISCOVERY OF
TUTANKHAMEN'S
—TOMB—

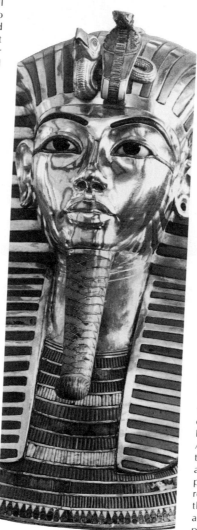

West of Thebes, in Egypt, on **25th November 1922,** the first stone **was removed** from the wall closing the entrance to Tutankhamen's tomb, and Howard Carter, the archaeologist who **had discovered** it, together with his patron and friend, Lord Carnarvon, and Lord Carnarvon's daughter, **were able to see** for the first time the most incredible buried treasure that has ever been known.

Carter **had** first **come** to Egypt 30 years before, in **1892.** For several years he **had been** a draughtsman assisting two other archaeologists, Davis and Maspero, **until** in **1903,** he **was appointed** Archaeological Inspector of Lower and Middle Egypt. The turning point in his life **came,** however, in **1907,** when Maspero **introduced** him to Lord Carnarvon, a rich aristocrat who **had just arrived** in Egypt. Lord Carnarvon was impressed by his qualities, and from **1908-12** they **explored** the western region of Thebes together, on the left bank of the Nile.

At this time, the name of Tutankhamen **was** almost unknown. Davis **had found** a few objects referring to him in the Valley of the Kings, near Thebes, in **1906-7,** but in **1909** he **had abandoned** the search because the contents of the subterranean chamber where he **had made** his finds were badly damaged, and he felt that the treasure of the Valley of the Kings was now exhausted. Maspero, however, did not agree, and it was because of Maspero's theories that Carter eventually **made** a systematic exploration of much of the western sector of the Valley from **1919-21** and reached the conclusion that the tomb of Tutankhamen must lie between those of Rameses III and Rameses VI.

In the intervening years, he **had left** the area for a time, moving north to dig in the Nile Delta at Sais in **1912** and only resuming work near Thebes in **1914,** when cobras, the snakes sacred to the ancient Egyptians, **had** literally **driven** the diggers from the other site. **Subsequently,** his work **had been held up** by the First World War.

By November 1922, Carter **had** almost **given up** hope, and Lord Carnarvon in England **had begun** to wonder if any important discovery would ever be made. But on **the morning of November 4th,** digging under Rameses VI's tomb, Carter **saw** what looked like the beginning of a step cut in the rock. It was followed by others that led to a screen of stones plastered over and bearing the seals of a royal burial place. After sixteen steps, a name could be seen: Nebkheprure-Tutankhamen. **Three weeks later,** when Lord Carnarvon and his daughter **had arrived** from England, the tomb **was opened.** After Carter's first, quick glance, the patron was able to see strange animals, statues and gold. His patience and faith in Carter were rewarded, and for Carter himself the sight was a crowning achievement after 30 years of perseverance and hard work.

● **Activity 2**

Compare this account with the one on the opposite page.

1 Make notes on the content of each paragraph here to see how it differs from the first although the information contained is the same.

2 Note the uses of the Past Perfect (**had** + past participle) to provide incidental information which helps to explain the main, important events, which are always given in the Past Simple.

A modern treasure hunt

Treasure hunts have occupied people's imagination for hundreds of years both in real life — for example, the search for Eldorado — and in books such as Robert Louis Stevenson's *Treasure Island*. Kit Williams, a modern author, had the idea of combining the real excitement of a treasure hunt with clues found in a book when he **published** a very popular children's story, *Masquerade*, in 1979. The book was about a hare, and a month before it was published Williams buried a gold hare, studded with jewels, in a park in Bedfordshire. The book contained a large number of clues in words and pictures to help readers find the hare, but Williams put in a lot of 'red herrings', or false clues,

to mislead them. In February 1982, the hare **was** finally **found**. In the meantime, over a million people **had bought** the book and thousands had spent hours searching for the hare.

Ken Roberts, the man who found the hare, **had been looking for** it for nearly two years. Although he had been searching in the wrong area for most of the time, he eventually **found** it by logic, not by luck. His success derived from the fact that he **had solved** an important clue at the start. He had realised that the words: 'One of Six to Eight' under the first picture in the book connected the hare in some way to Katherine of Aragon, the first of Henry VIII's six wives. Even here, however, Williams had succeeded in

...sleading him. Ken knew that
...atherine of Aragon **had died** at
...mbolton in Cambridgeshire in 1536
...d assumed that Williams **had
...ried** the hare in the grounds of the
...stle. He **had been digging** there for
...er a year and had twice given up in
...gust before a new idea **occurred** to
...m. He found out that Kit Williams
...d **spent** his childhood near
...mpthill, in Bedfordshire, and
...asoned that he must have buried the
...re in a place he knew well, but he
...l could not see the connection with
...atherine of Aragon, until one day he
...me across two stone crosses in
...mpthill Park and learnt that they
...d **been erected** in her honour in
...73.
...Even then his search had not come
...an end. It was only after he **had
...ent** several nights digging around
...e cross that he decided to write to Kit
...lliams to find out if he was wasting
...time there. Williams **encouraged
...m** to continue, and on February 24th
...32, he found the treasure. He **had**, in
...t, he afterwards discovered, **dug up
...e** hare in its protective covering
...eviously in the dark and reburied it
...thout realising it. On March 12th,
...n, accompanied by Kit Williams,
...mber Gascoigne, who **had acted** as
...lliams's witness when the hare was
...ginally buried, and a BBC television
...w, finally melted down the wax
...ding the mould around the hare
...d **unwrapped** it. It had originally
...en worth £3000, but the excitement
...**ad caused** since its burial made it
...ch more valuable as a souvenir ■

● **Activity 3**

This story is written so that the narrative
emphasises the important facts but sometimes
refers back to others. Put as precise a date
(or dates — **from... to...**) as you can against
the actions referred to in each of the verbs in
bold type.

The article below has been printed with the paragraphs and sentences in each paragraph out of order. Reorder them so that they make a logical, continuous narrative. Look for a paragraph defining the topic to begin with and then find words relating to subsequent paragraphs.

The Search for Eldorado

1 a) This exaggeration was convenient to the Indians, who hoped to get rid of the white men by telling them that Eldorado was a little further on. b) At first the explorers confined their search to the highlands around Bogota, but when they found nothing there, the search spread to the Orinoco and Amazon valleys. c) It was also useful to the Viceroy of Peru, who encouraged some of the dangerous adventurers around him to take part in the quest. d) By this time the legend had grown to suggest an entire country of gold.

2 a) In recent years, Aguirre's mutiny has been turned into an interesting film by the German director, Werner Herzog. b) The colonial governors were ordered to hunt him down, and he eventually killed himself after they had defeated him in battle. c) After this the authorities were determined to arrest him.

3 a) The tribal chief was covered from head to foot in gum and powdered gold was blown over him until he looked like a golden statue. b) At the end of the ceremony, he led his people to the shores of Lake Guatavita and dived in to wash away the gold dust and so cleanse the tribe of sin. c) The search for El Dorado, which in Spanish means 'the Gilded One', began because of a ceremony held every year by an Indian tribe in the highlands of Colombia.

● Composition

1 Tell the story of an important historical event.
2 Tell the story of how something valuable was found, either as it appeared in the news or as an account of something that happened in your family.
3 Tell the story of a journey you made involving difficulties.

4 a) He began a reign of terror among them and had several executed before leading them eventually to Margarita, a Spanish settlement on an island off the coast of Venezuela, which they destroyed. b) The most dangerous of all was Lope de Aguirre, who led a mutiny against his young commander on one of these expeditions in 1561 and killed him and his wife. c) Once the murder was done, however, Aguirre's associates realised they had chosen a madman for their leader.

5 a) Although not all the colonists believed it, the enormous wealth the Spaniards had found in Peru suggested that it might be true. b) In the legend the Gilded Man was a king who lived in a golden city and whose soldiers wore golden armour. c) The ceremony had stopped about 1480, a few years before Columbus arrived in America, but it became the basis of an Indian legend.

Prescribed books: Relationships between characters

24

Checklist

● **So and such (2)**

See Unit 14 Checklist.

The following variation is acceptable but generally considered rather old-fashioned.

Mr Bennet was **so odd a mixture** of sarcastic humour, reserve and caprice. (from Jane Austen)
Mr Bennet was **such an odd mixture** of...(normal modern construction)
I wish I could say... that the accomplishment of her earnest desire... produced **so happy an effect** as to make her a sensible, amiable, well-informed woman. (from Jane Austen)
I wish I could say... that the accomplishment of her earnest desire... produced **such a happy effect** as to make her... (normal modern construction)

24.1 In drama

You may be asked to describe the relationships between characters in a play such as Robert Bolt's *A Man for All Seasons*. A typical question might be:

Describe More's relationship with one of the following: King Henry, Richard Rich, the Duke of Norfolk.

In preparing for such questions, remember that in most modern plays the dramatist describes the characters in a preface or in stage directions, and frequently indicates the relationships between them by saying how the actors should speak the lines. Supposing that in this case you decided to write about More's relationship with Richard Rich, you could have prepared beforehand by noting: 1) the dramatist's comments; 2) each of Rich's appearances as part of a general synopsis of the play; 3) crucial lines affecting the relationship between More and Rich.

● Character

'RICHARD RICH: Early 30s. A studious, unhappy face lit by the fire of banked down (= controlled) appetite. He is an academic hounded (= pursued) by self-doubt to be in the world of affairs (= of politics) and longing to be rescued from himself'. (Robert Bolt)

● Appearances

1 Accepts a cup from More, intended as a bribe in a law suit. Wishes to befriend More to get a political appointment. More advises him to be a schoolmaster and gets him a job as the Duke of Norfolk's librarian.
2 Now the Duke's secretary. Meets Cromwell (later More's successor).
3 Shows when he visits More's house that he has become a spy for Cromwell.
4 Cromwell terrifies Rich and gains support.
5 Discusses the cup More gave him with Cromwell and Norfolk.
6 More is in prison. Rich is Cromwell's assistant when More is interrogated.
7 Swears false evidence against More at the trial. As a result, More is convicted and executed.

● Stage directions and quotations

RICH: (*enthusiastically pursuing an argument*) But every man has his price!...

RICH: (*bitterly disappointed*) A teacher!...

MORE: (*pleased*) Good...Well, you don't need my help now.
RICH: Sir Thomas, if only you knew how much, much rather I'd yours than his (i.e. Cromwell's).

MORE: (*gently*) Why Richard, have you done something that should make you not welcome? (in More's house)

CROMWELL: Sir Richard is appointed Attorney-General for Wales.
MORE: (*looking into Rich's face: with pain and amusement*) For Wales? Why, Richard, it profits a man nothing to give his soul for the whole world...But for Wales...!

Synopsis for information

A Man for All Seasons begins just before Sir Thomas More succeeded Wolsey as Chancellor (= Prime Minister) under Henry VIII in 1530. It shows how More, a devout Catholic, is forced to choose, first, between accepting the King's decision to break with Rome and make himself head of the Church of England, and obeying his conscience; later, between publicly acknowledging the legality of the King's divorce from his first wife, Katharine of Aragon, and remarriage with Anne Boleyn, and being executed for his beliefs. More is eventually executed, but he does not welcome martyrdom; on the contrary, throughout the play he uses his training as a lawyer to avoid committing himself openly; however, after attempts have failed to prove him corrupt or disloyal, he is convicted on the basis of false evidence given by Richard Rich.

Activity 1

1 Study the way in which the notes on the synopsis, the stage directions and quotations have been used in the composition.
2 Which phrases or sentences in the composition refer to the action of the play in order to explain the relationship, and which refer to the relationship itself?

24.2 In the novel

● **Plot outline**

Pride and Prejudice (Jane Austen)

Mr and Mrs Bennet have five daughters. On Mr Bennet's death, however, his estate must pass by law to the nearest male relative, the girls' cousin, Mr Collins, a clergyman. A rich young man, Mr Bingley, becomes their neighbour and falls in love with the eldest, Jane, but his even richer friend, Mr Darcy, believes she is not serious, and the two men leave for London. Meanwhile, the heroine, Elizabeth, the second daughter, has refused Mr Collins.

Darcy has been attracted to Elizabeth against his will, and, when they meet in Kent, proposes. She refuses him. Apart from blaming him for Jane's unhappiness, she has been prejudiced against him by a young officer, Mr Wickham, who complained that Darcy treated him badly, ignoring his father's will in Wickham's favour. In fact, as Elizabeth later discovers, Wickham is a fortune-hunter whose plan is to seduce girls and then blackmail their families into paying him to marry them. He failed with Darcy's sister, but succeeds with Lydia Bennet, the youngest daughter. His debts are paid and he marries her, apparently through the influence of Elizabeth's uncle, but really because of Darcy's intervention. In the end, Jane marries Bingley, and Elizabeth, now in love with Darcy, accepts him.

● **Useful quotations**

Characters: Mr Bennet — 'so odd a mixture of sarcastic humour, reserve and caprice'.
Mrs Bennet — 'a woman of mean understanding, little information, and uncertain temper. When she was discontented she fancied herself nervous. The business of her life was to get her daughters married.'

● **Relationship**

Mr Bennet, 'captivated by youth and beauty ... had married a woman whose weak understanding and illiberal mind had very early in their marriage put an end to all real affection for her'. 'To his wife he was very little... indebted than (= except in so far) as her ignorance and folly had contributed to his amusement.'

● **Judgements**

'Elizabeth...had never been blind to the impropriety of her father's behaviour as a husband...which, in exposing his wife to the contempt of her own children, was so highly reprehensible.'

The narrator (on Mrs Bennet, at the end of the novel): 'I wish I could say, for the sake of her family, that the accomplishment of her earnest desire in the establishment of so many of her children produced so happy an effect as to make her a sensible, amiable, well-informed woman.'

A typical question on *Pride and Prejudice* might be:
Illustrate the relationship between Mr and Mrs Bennet and comment on its effect on their daughters.

Assuming you had read the book and made a synopsis of each chapter and character notes, you could plan a composition taking into account the statements on the opposite page, and these relevant events: Mr Bennet amuses himself at his wife's expense, pretending he does not know of Bingley's arrival (1) and laughs at her horror that Collins will get the estate (23). When Elizabeth refuses Collins (20), he is pleased, his wife horrified; he realises his irresponsibility when Lydia elopes, while his wife blames everyone but herself (47). He worries, thinking that Elizabeth is going to marry Darcy for his money, while his wife regards this as the main attraction (59).

(The numbers in brackets in the paragraph above refer to chapters in the novel.)

1 Characters of Mr and Mrs Bennet and their relationship.
2 Mrs Bennet's example and its effect on her daughters.
3 Mr Bennet's irresponsibility.
4 Author's conclusion

● Activity 2

Find the basis for statements made in the composition in the information given opposite. Study the use of relevant events, character analysis and quotations from the text.

Question: Illustrate the relationship between Mr and Mrs Bennet and comment on its effect on their daughters.

It is difficult to understand why Mr Bennet married his wife, because he is so intelligent and she is so silly. Apparently he was attracted by her youth and beauty and did not trouble to get to know her well. This irresponsibility has continued since their marriage; instead of trying to teach her common sense, he makes her a victim of his 'sarcastic humour'. When the novel begins he pretends he does not know of Bingley's arrival in the neighbourhood, and he laughs at her genuine concern that Mr Collins will inherit the estate.

Mrs Bennet is clearly described in the first chapter: 'The business of her life was to get her daughters married.' But she is herself the main obstacle to her own ambition. She is rude to Darcy and absurdly polite to Bingley. If she had had her way, Elizabeth would have had to marry Mr Collins. She does not realise that her bad example is the reason why Kitty and Lydia only think of young officers and why Lydia runs off with Wickham. She is as happy about that marriage, where the husband is a blackmailer, as about the others.

Although Mr Bennet is very entertaining, he shares the blame for Lydia's behaviour, and Elizabeth, his favourite, wishes he had treated her mother better and educated her younger sisters. He himself later realises his irresponsibility when he realises he cannot repay his brother-in-law (though Darcy, of course, was really the one who saved Lydia). Unlike his wife, however, he has a sense of values and will not consent to Elizabeth marrying Darcy until she convinces him that they really love one another.

Jane Austen herself clearly regards the Bennets' marriage as a failure and a warning. The point of the book is that Elizabeth and Darcy will be much happier because they have learnt to understand each other, overcoming pride and prejudice, where Mr Bennet committed himself much too soon for inadequate reasons.

24.3 Choosing your hero

● Activity 3

Before reading the text below, decide, if you have seen any of the films listed below, which character you found more interesting:

Wyatt Earp or Doc Holliday in *Gunfight at OK Corral.*
Butch Cassidy or The Sundance Kid in *Butch Cassidy and The Sundance Kid.*
Luke Skywalker or Han Solo in *Star Wars.*
The husband or the wife in *On Golden Pond.*
Harold Abrahams or Eric Liddell in *Chariots of Fire.*

This sort of question in a composition about a prescribed book is a trap. It is very likely if you chose the first character in the first three questions above that you happen to find Burt Lancaster more attractive than Kirk Douglas, Paul Newman more interesting than Robert Redford, and Mark Hamill more exciting than Harrison Ford, or vice versa if you chose the second character. Your choice in the fourth may depend on your sympathy for Henry Fonda or Katharine Hepburn, rather than the parts they were playing; your choice for the last is perhaps influenced by whether you admire the determination of Harold Abrahams more than the religious integrity of Eric Liddell. In all cases, you should consider instead the intentions of the film director, who in these particular films either wanted you to sympathise with both characters in different ways, or, in the case of *Star Wars*, knew that characters would appeal to different people in the audience.

It is very unwise (because it suggests an uncritical attitude) to say that you like a character in a book or play because you happen to prefer people with certain characteristics in real life. In *Gone with the Wind* most of us would be happier being married to Melanie Hamilton (Olivia de Havilland) than Scarlett O'Hara (Vivien Leigh), but Scarlett is the centre of attention. What matters is whether you understand the writer's intentions and can say whether the character is consistent in the book and realistic in terms of your experience of life.

● Activity 4

Consider the characters in the book or play you are reading. List the aspects of their character that you find attractive or interesting. Do you think your response to them is what the author intended? If so, why? If not, why not? Then discuss your conclusions with other members of the class.

● Composition

Describe the relationship between any two characters in the novel or play you are reading.

Reference section

Grammatical reference

- **Definite article**

1 Omission of the

We do not use **the** with the following:

a) Games and sports

I **play football** every week. My sister **plays tennis** and **likes swimming**, too.

b) Subjects of study

I **studied literature** at university and now I **teach English**.

c) Languages

Many Welsh people **speak Welsh**, but most Scots **speak English**.

Note that we can say **the English** (noun) or **English people**, but nationality as an adjective has no definite or indefinite article.

I'm English.

d) Meals and clock time

What time do you **have breakfast**?
— **About eight o'clock**.

e) Gerunds

Horse-racing is more popular in Britain than **fox-hunting**.

f) Collocations (preposition + noun)

Notice that there is no **the** after the preposition in these sentences:

Is he still **in bed**?
— No, he's **at church**.
 I was **at school** for thirteen years and then I went **to university**.

A number of common phrases in English made up of a preposition and a noun do not take **the**.

Here is a list of the most common ones:

bed (**in, to**)	market (**at, to**)
church (**at, in** = inside, **to**)	paper (**on**)
court (**in, to**)	prison (**in, to**)
dock (**in**)	school (**at, to**)
harbour (**in, to**)	sea (**at, to**)
home (**at**)	university (**at, to**)
hospital (**in, to**)	work (**at, to**)

The definite article is only used when we clearly refer to a particular school, hospital, etc.

My mother's **in hospital**.
I'm going **to the hospital** this afternoon to take her some flowers.

Modes of travel and transport take **by** + noun, without **the**.

By air/sea/road
By car/bus/plane/train, etc.

Note that we say **on foot**.

2 Use of the

We use **the** with the following:

a) Weights and measures

Petrol is sold **by the litre**.

b) Groups or classes of people

The young often get impatient with their parents.

We can say either **the young** or **young people**. The verb that follows expressions of this kind is plural.

c) Rivers, seas, mountain ranges

The Amazon is longer than **the River Thames**.
The Mediterranean flows into **the Atlantic Ocean**.
Mount Everest is the highest mountain in **the Himalayas**.

Note that we use **the** in all cases, except for the name of a single mountain,

Mount Everest, Kilimanjaro.

d) Unique objects, points of the compass, some time expressions

The sun rises in **the east**.
The past is often more real to old people than **the present**.

We use **the** when there is only one of something:

the sun, the moon, the earth, the world.

We use **the** with points of the compass:

the north, the south, the east, the west.

But compare these sentences:

We were travelling **north**.
We were travelling **towards the north**.

We usually use **the** when we speak of **the past, the present** and **the future**. The exceptions are **at present**, which means 'now, at this time' and **in future**, which means 'from now on'.

I'll drive more carefully **in future** (from now on, from this moment).
In the future (but not from now on) men may live on the moon.

3 Use and omission of the

We use **the** when we are talking about something *specific*.
We don't use **the** when we are speaking in a more *general* sense.

a) Plural count nouns and mass nouns

She likes **flowers**. (General)
She liked **the flowers** that I gave her. (Specific)
Coffee is expensive nowadays. (General)
The coffee that you bought is very bitter. (Specific)

b) Abstract nouns

I always admire **honesty**. (General)
I was surprised at **the honesty** with which he answered the questions. (Specific)

c) Species of animals

Elephants are said to have long memories.

When we talk about animals in general, we usually use the plural without **the**.
When we refer to a particular species we can use either **the** and a singular noun,

The Indian elephant is smaller than **the African elephant**.

or a plural noun without **the**,

Indian elephants are smaller than **African elephants**.

d) Noun + modifying phrase/clause

Life is always valuable.
Modern life is often tiring.
Albert Schweitzer's life was devoted to the sick.
The life he is leading bores him.
The life of our grandparents was very different from the life we lead today.

The is used when the noun is modified by a relative clause, or by a phrase including **of**.

● Adjectives: comparison

1 One-syllable and three-syllable adjectives

He's **taller** than his sister; in fact, he's **the tallest** in the family.
But she's **more intelligent** than he is. She's **the most intelligent** person I've ever met.

One-syllable adjectives form the comparative with **-er** and the superlative with **-est**; adjectives with three syllables or more form the comparative with **more** and the superlative with **most**.
Note the irregular forms: **good, better, best; bad, worse, worst**.

2 Two-syllable adjectives

That house is **prettier** than the last one we looked at; in fact, I think it's **the prettiest** we've seen so far.
Cathy is **more cheerful** than her sister; actually she's **the most cheerful** person I know.

Two-syllable adjectives usually form the comparative with **more** and the superlative with **most**. But an important group, those ending in **-y** (e.g. **happy, easy, lucky**), form the comparative with **-er** and the superlative with **-est**. Note that the **-y** changes to **i** (e.g. **happier, happiest**).

Other groups taking **-er** and **-est** are those ending in **-le** (e.g. **noble, gentle**), **-ow** (e.g. **narrow, yellow**) and **-er** (e.g. **clever, tender**).

All others (e.g. those ending in **-ful, -less**, such as **cheerful, useless**), usually take **more** and **most**.

In a few cases (e.g. **common, stupid, unfair, unkind, pleasant**), both the **-er/-est** and **more/most** forms are found.

● Adjectives: word order

It is difficult to give clear rules to follow about the position of adjectives before the noun. The table below, however, should be of value as a useful check in given cases. The following general points should also be remembered:

1 When there are more than two adjectives, they are usually linked by commas.

2 We seldom use **and** except when the adjectives are a complement, following **be**:

His work is untidy **and** unsatisfactory.

3 We usually put the more or most precise adjective nearest the noun but it is not always easy to decide which is more precise. When in doubt, consult the examples and order given below:

All the first three competitors broke the record. (1,2,3,4)
The beautiful, intelligent girl fell in love with **the tall young** man. (2,5,6 and 2,7,8)
There was a **round, green** spot on **the carved, wooden Japanese** screen. (9,10 and 2,11,12, 13)
He had a **beautiful, old, ivory chess** piece. (5, 8,12,14)

  1) **both, all** or **half**
  2) **the**

3) Ordinal number (**first, last**)
4) Cardinal number (**one, three**)
5) General judgement (**good, bad, nice, beautiful**)
6) General judgement (mental — **intelligent, stupid**)
7) Measurement (**big, tall**)
8) Age or temperature (**old, young, hot**)
9) Shape (**round, square**)
10) Colour (**red, green**)
11) Verb participle form (**carved, boiling**)
12) Material (**wooden**)
13) Origin, nationality (**French, Mediterranean**)
14) Noun in apposition (**steel, cigarette**)

Some of these categories are reversed at times, particularly the following:

6 and 7 for emphasis on 6. In this case, the comma must always be used.

A **little, intelligent** man (7,6)

10 and 13 in a phrase like:

Yugoslavian white wine. (13,10)

Here **white** is used to describe a type, in contrast to **red**, rather than as an indication of colour.

● **It's + adjective + for/that**

It's easy (for you) to say that.
It's obvious that you don't know what you're talking about.

In some cases, the adjective may be followed by either construction but usually we prefer one or the other. Among the adjectives followed by **for** are: **boring, dangerous, difficult, easy, expensive, healthy, necessary**.

Among those followed by **that** are: **certain, clear, curious, likely, lucky, probable, surprising, true**. Note the use of **interesting** with the two constructions:

It would be interesting for you to study abroad. (You would find it interesting.)
It's interesting that he made you that offer. (I find it interesting.)

● **Adverbs: word order**

1 Adverbs of frequency (**often, always, usually**, etc.)
  a) **Be** (including negatives and passives)

  The opposite **is usually** the case.
  He **isn't often** late.
  Headlines **are often designed** to puzzle the reader.

  b) **Be** with auxiliary (including negatives and passives)

  He **has always been** very kind to me.
  They **may not always be** the best newspapers for foreign students.
  I **have never been asked** a question like that before.

  c) Other verbs (including negatives and one auxiliary)

  It **often confuses** foreigners.
  I **don't usually look at** my mail till after breakfast.
  He **has always taken** a great personal interest in my career.

  d) Other verbs with two auxiliaries

  I **could never have done** it without your help.

Adverbs of Manner, Place and Time

	SUBJECT	VERB	OBJECT	ADVERBIAL
HOW	I	miss	him	**very much.**
WHERE	They	haven't got	a man	**around the house.**
WHEN	They	had fallen off	a boat	**while they were playing.**

(WHEN)		HOW	WHERE	WHEN
	She acted	**terribly**	**in the film.**	
(Yesterday)	The film fans besieged the airport	**frantically**		**yesterday.**
(An hour later)	I interviewed him		**in his flat**	**an hour later.**

a) Time expressions (WHEN) can come at the beginning or end of the sentence. We usually put them at the beginning if the time expression or the sentence is very long, or for emphasis.

b) We sometimes put one-word adverbs of manner (HOW) in front of the main verb for emphasis — in the example above, we could say:

The film fans frantically besieged the airport.

c) We usually put the adverb of place (WHERE) before the adverb of manner (HOW) after verbs of movement:

She went to London (WHERE) by train (HOW) yesterday (WHEN).

● **Prepositions**

1 Prepositions of place

at, in

At is used for particular points, **in** for larger areas.

He was waiting **at** the bus stop.
He is staying **at** the Ritz Hotel.
She lives **in** London.
There are a lot of mountains **in** Switzerland.

Confusion is only possible when the point of view of the speaker is different.

Someone who lives in a city may say:

My friend, Mary, lives **at** Farley. (a small village)

but a farmer who lives outside the village may say:

Mary lives **in** Farley.

In the same way, a housewife answering the phone may say:

My husband's **at** his office. (= at his place of work)

but his secretary, sitting outside the office, may say to a visitor:

Mr Jones is **in** his office. I'll tell him you're here.

in, out, on, off, into, out of, on to

Notice the prepositions in these sentences:

Look, there's a boat **on** the lake. (floating on the surface)
He's **in** the water. (swimming)
He took his hat **off**. (It was on his head.)
The dentist took my tooth **out**. (It was in my head.)

He got **into** the car. He got **on to** his bicycle.
He fell **out of** his pram. He fell **off** the roof.

In almost always suggests 'inside' in English; **on** means 'on the surface of'.

Out is the opposite of **in**, and **off** is the opposite of **on**. With verbs of movement, when there is an object, we use **into** and **out of**, **on to** and **off**.

We say **get on** and **get off** for a bus and **get in** and **get out of** for a train,

You must **get out** at the next station. (train)
You must **get off** at the next stop. (bus)

This is because buses did not have closing doors until recently in Britain.
We would normally use **get out of** for a coach, because coaches have always had doors.

On or **at the corner** is used for corners outside (of a street, for example).
In is used for corners inside (of a room, for example).

opposite, in front of

Opposite is often confused with **in front of**. Compare:

I asked the woman sitting **in front of** me at the cinema to take her hat off. (We were both facing in the same direction.)
I sat **opposite** my wife at the table. (facing her)

2 Prepositions of time

at

Exact points of time — **at 5 o'clock, at dinner time, at this moment.**
Festivals — **at Christmas, at Easter, at New Year.**
At night, (but: **during the day**), **at weekends, at the weekend.**

on

Days and dates — **on Monday, on June 10th, on Christmas Day, on a summer evening, on a Sunday morning, on Wednesday night.**

in

Longer periods of time — **in August, in spring, in 1968, in the twentieth century, in the Middle Ages, in the past, in the future.**
Periods of time within which or at the end of which something may happen — **in five minutes, in three years' time.**
In the morning, in the afternoon, in the evening.

by

By = 'at some time not later than'.

I'll pay you **at** the end of the month. (on the 30th or 31st)
I'll pay you **by** the end of the month. (perhaps during the month at any time, but certainly not later than the 31st)

3 Some useful time expressions

At first, in the beginning (not used for points in argument — *see Connecters and Modifiers, page 160*).
In the end, finally (The first is not used for points in argument.)
Eventually = after a long period of time.
At last comes at the end of a long series of events.
For the time being = until things change.
In the meantime = meanwhile.
In due course = in the future, at the proper time.
Now and then = from time to time (at irregular intervals).
These days = at the present time.
In those days refers to the past.
Nowadays refers to the present in contrast to the past.
At the moment = now; **at this moment** may mean 'now' but may mean the time being referred to.
At present/at the present time = now, but **presently** (in British English) = soon.

● Modals: Formulae for different situations

All phrases we use here are polite but we have indicated differences, where necessary, between what you normally say to a friend (informal, marked **I** in the left-hand margin); what you say formally to someone you know (formal, marked **F**); and what you say to someone you do not know (very formal, marked **VF**). On the right-hand side we have given appropriate answers to the question formulae in the examples.

Remember that the relationships between people in a society affect the formality of the language they use. In general, for example, secretaries are more polite and formal towards their bosses than bosses towards their secretaries; shop assistants are more polite and formal towards customers than customers towards shop assistants. This is not always true, but it is a good rule to remember.

1 You want someone (not) to do something.

I   **Help me** with these cases, will you?
Will/Can you help me with these cases, please?
Would/Could you help me with these cases, (please)?

(The last is the most polite.)

Please don't make a noise. The baby's asleep. (Negative)

All right.
Yes, of course.
Certainly.
I'm sorry. I can't.
I'm very sorry, but...

F   **I want you to** help me.
I'd like you to help me.

(The second is more polite.)

I don't want you to make the same mistake again. (Negative)

Yes, of course./Certainly. What can I do?
I'm terribly sorry, but...

VF **Would you mind** helping me with these cases?
Would you mind not smoking in the waiting room? (Negative)

Yes, of course.
Certainly.
I'm sorry, I didn't realise.

2 You are asking permission to do something.

I   **Can/May I** borrow the car, please?
Could I borrow the car, please?

(The second is more polite, or you are less sure that the person will say 'Yes'.)

All right.
Yes, of course.
Certainly.
I'm sorry, but....

F   **Do you mind if I** open the window?
Would you mind if I opened the window?

(Again, the second is more polite, or you are less sure that the person will say 'Yes'.)

No, not at all.
Well, I'd rather you didn't. I...

3 You are offering something to someone.

I   **Do you want** some tea?
    Do you want to watch TV?
I/F **Would you like** some tea?
    Would you like to watch TV?

$\left\{\begin{array}{l}\text{Yes, please.}\\ \text{No, thanks. (I'd rather...)}\end{array}\right.$

4 You are offering to do something.

I   **Do you want me to** help you with the washing-up?
I/F **Shall I** help you with the washing-up?
    Would you like me to help you with the washing-up?
VF **Can I** help you?

(This is used as a formula in shops, etc.)

$\left\{\begin{array}{l}\text{Oh, yes. Thank you.}\\ \text{No, that's all right, thanks.}\end{array}\right.$

$\left\{\begin{array}{l}\text{Yes, actually I'm looking}\\ \text{for...}\\ \text{No, thank you. I'd just like}\\ \text{to look around.}\end{array}\right.$

5 You are suggesting something you want to do with the other person.

I   **Shall we** go to London this weekend?
    How about going to London this weekend?
    Why don't we go to London this weekend?
    Let's go to London this weekend.

(Each is more positive than the one before. The last is not a question.)

In making suggestions to solve problems (F), the second and third are the most common.)

$\left\{\begin{array}{l}\text{Yes. That's a good idea.}\\ \text{Well, I'd rather not...}\\ \text{Well, I think we should...}\end{array}\right.$

6 You are suggesting something to the other person or trying to advise him/her.

Why don't you go to the doctor?
Why not go to the doctor?

(These phrases show less concern than those below.)

Don't you think you should/ought to go to the doctor?
I think you should/ought to/had better go to the doctor.
You should go to the doctor.
You'd better go to the doctor.

$\left\{\begin{array}{l}\text{Yes, all right. I will.}\\ \text{Yes, I suppose I should.}\\ \text{Well, I don't think I need}\\ \text{to.}\end{array}\right.$

(Each is stronger and more urgent than the other one before.)

Note: 'You **ought to** go to the doctor' usually suggests 'but I don't suppose you will.'

7 You are giving orders or explaining obligations.

a) Positive forms:

Write your name in ink.
You **must** write your name in ink.

(The second is an explanation, not an order.)

You **have to** write your name in ink.

(The speaker is not responsible for the rule.)

You **should** write your name in ink.

(The speaker is only giving advice; see 6 above.)

b) Negative forms (prohibition):

Don't drive so fast! You're breaking the speed limit.
You **mustn't** drive so fast. You're breaking the speed limit. (It is against the law.)
You **shouldn't** drive so fast. You'll have an accident one day. (It is not necessarily against the law.) (The speaker is giving advice, not an order.)

c) You are telling someone that there is no obligation:

You **needn't** write in ink (if you don't want to).
You **don't have to** write in ink.

Note: See 9 below for past forms.

8 You are explaining your own obligations or prohibitions to someone else.

a) Obligations:

I **must** give up smoking. It's bad for my health.
I **have to** give up smoking. I don't want to, but the doctor says it will kill me.
I **should** give up smoking. I know it's bad for me, but I find it difficult to stop.

Note: It is polite to say 'I **have to** go now' when you say goodbye to someone, because it suggests that you don't want to go. The obligation comes from outside.

b) Prohibitions:

I **mustn't** smoke. I've got a bad cold.

c) You have no obligation:

I **needn't** go to work tomorrow. They've given us a holiday.
I **haven't got to** go to work tomorrow. They've given us a holiday.

Note: **I don't have to** (see 7) is usually used in general terms.

I **don't have to** go to work on Saturdays.

9 Past forms expressing obligation and prohibition.

a) Obligation:

We **had to** walk home because our car broke down.

b) Prohibition (see 7b and 8b):

We **weren't allowed to** stay up late when I was young.
We **couldn't** stay up late when I was young.

c) There was no obligation (see 7c and 8c):

We **didn't need to** book the tickets in advance. It wasn't a very popular film.

Note: 'We **needn't have** booked the tickets in advance.' This means that we booked the tickets, but it wasn't necessary.

10 You are complaining about someone or blaming him/her.

Why didn't you shut the gate?
You should have shut the gate.
Why did you park your car there?
You shouldn't have parked your car there.

{ I'm sorry. I didn't
think (realise).
I did (didn't).
It's not my fault.

11 You are wondering about something and thinking about possible explanations (Present).

Situation: You are in the street outside a church. A wedding is going to take place and you are waiting to see the bride arrive. A man about 60 years old arrives and someone asks, 'Who's that?'

a) Possibilities:

He **may be** one of the guests.
He **could be** the best man.
He **might be** the bridegroom.

(The first is a reasonable possibility. The second is possible but not likely — the man is old. The third is possible but very unlikely for the same reason.)

b) Negative forms:

He **may not be** one of the guests. He may be a stranger, like us.
He **might not be** one of the guests, but he's talking to the other people there.

c) Logical conclusions:

He **must know** the bridegroom. Look! He's shaking hands with him.
He **can't be** one of the guests. He's going away. (Negative)
He **couldn't be** one of the guests. He's wearing an old suit. (Negative)

(In the last example, the conclusion is not clear. You are saying, 'I can't believe it'.)

Note: If you are wondering about people's actions, use the same forms with Continuous tenses.

He **may/could/might be working** late this evening. That's why he hasn't arrived.

12 You are wondering about something and thinking of possible events (Future).

Question: Is it going to rain tonight?

a) Possibilities:

It **may** rain. It often does at this time of year.
It **might** rain, but I don't think it will.

b) Negative forms:

Don't look so sad. It **may not** rain this evening.
It **might not** rain tonight but the sky looks very dark.

13 You are wondering about something that (has) happened and thinking of possible explanations (Past).

Problem: What (has) happened to your umbrella?

a) Possibilities:

I **may have** left it at the office.
Someone **might have** borrowed it.

(The second is possible, but you don't think this is the explanation.)

Note: We normally use **could have** when someone has not taken advantage of a possibility. See 10 above, but you are not complaining or blaming the other person.

Why did you come by train? You **could have** come by air.

b) Negative forms:

I **may not have** left it at the office. I may have left it on the train. Of course I **might not have** taken it to the office this morning, but I'm sure I did.

c) Logical conclusions:

Now I remember. I had it when I got off the train but I bought some cigarettes on the way home. I **must have** left it in the tobacconist's shop.
I **can't have** left it anywhere else. (Negative)

Note: The difference between **can't have** and **couldn't have** in the negative is not very clear, but the first suggests 'I'm sure he hasn't' and the second 'I'm sure he didn't'.

He **can't have** seen the letter. It's still on his desk and he hasn't opened it.
He **couldn't have** seen the letter. He was on holiday when it arrived.

14 You are telling someone that you know how to do something, or you have the physical ability to do something.

a) Present forms:

I **can** play the piano but I **can't** play the violin.
I **can** run 100 metres in 11 seconds but I **can't** run as fast as John.

b) Past forms:

I **could** speak French when I was ten but I **couldn't** speak English.
He **could** throw a ball a long way but he **couldn't** catch very well.

c) Future forms:

I**'ll be able to** speak English quite well when I go to England.
We **won't be able to** climb the mountain tomorrow. The weather isn't good enough.

15 You are telling someone that an action will (not) be possible or was (not) possible.

a) Future forms:

I **can (can't)** come to the meeting tomorrow.
I**'ll (I won't) be able to** come to the meeting tomorrow.

(The second is perhaps more polite and is better as an excuse, but there is not much difference.)

b) Past forms (Negative):

I **couldn't** go to the meeting yesterday. I was very busy.
I **wasn't able to** go to the meeting yesterday. I was very busy.

Note: In the affirmative, you say, 'I went to the meeting'. If you went but it was difficult because you were busy, see 16 below.

c) Present Perfect forms:

I**'ve been able to** work better since we moved to the country.
I'm sorry the job isn't finished. I've been ill, so I **haven't been able to** do anything.

16 You are telling someone that an action was difficult for you but you (finally) did it.

My car crashed and I hurt my leg, but I **was able to** get out and shout for help.
My car crashed and I hurt my leg, but I **managed to** get out and shout for help.

Note: If the action was too difficult (therefore impossible), use **couldn't** or **wasn't able to** (see 15b).

● Verbs not usually used in Continuous forms

Certain verbs are almost never found in continuous forms. They are mainly verbs connected with senses, mental processes, wishes, appearance and possession. Here is a list of the most common ones:

hear, notice, recognise, see, smell*, taste;
believe, feel (that), think (that)*;
know, mean, suppose, understand;
forget, remember*;
care, dislike, hate, love, want, wish;
appear (=seem), **seem;**
belong to, consist of, contain, have (=own, possess);
matter;
refuse.

*Note the following:

That **smells** good. (Intransitive)
She **is smelling** the rose. (Transitive)
What **do** you **think?** (What is your opinion?)
What **are** you **thinking?** (What thoughts are going through your mind?)
Do you **remember** our schooldays? (Have you any memory of them?)
Are you **remembering** our schooldays? (Are memories going through your mind?)

● Verb + gerund/infinitive

1 Gerund (only)
Some common verbs followed by a gerund are:
avoid, dislike, enjoy, finish, not mind, practise, can't help, can't stand.

Note: I **enjoy working** here.
I **can't understand him (his) working** so hard.

A gerund follows a verb + preposition.

He **kept on working**.

Note in particular the following, using the preposition **to:**
amount to, be (get) accustomed to, be given to, be opposed to, be (get) used to, come

near to, limit oneself to, look forward to, object to, resign oneself to.

2 Infinitive without **to**
Let and **make** take the infinitive without **to**.

Let him **go**.

Note: **Help** can be used with or without **to**.

Help him **(to) do** it.

Most auxiliary verbs: **can, must, had better,** etc.

Exceptions are **have to, ought to** and **used to**. (Compare **be used to, get used to** in 1.)

3 Verbs taking gerund and infinitive, including changes in meaning

allow	The doctor doesn't **allow me to smoke**. We don't **allow smoking** in the classroom. **Allow** takes an infinitive with a personal object, a gerund where there is none.
begin	I'**m beginning to feel** tired. **Begin** (and **start**) are not normally used with a gerund in continuous tenses (e.g. I'**m beginning**).
continue	(see **remember**)
forget **hate**	The gerund is the usual form, but the infinitive occurs: I **hate to interrupt** you while you're working. (I'm sorry to interrupt you.) I'**d hate to live** there, (Conditional form, see **like**).
intend **like** **love**	The gerund is used in general terms, meaning 'enjoy, find agreeable'. The infinitive is used when **like** means 'prefer'.

I **like** people **to be** polite.
I **like to have** a good breakfast before I go to work.

In the negative, when **don't like** means 'dislike' (see 1 above), **like** takes the gerund.
If it means 'I'm sorry to' (see **hate**), it takes the infinitive.
The Conditional form of **like** and **love** is followed by the infinitive (see **hate**).

I**'d like to go** home now.

prefer   I **prefer driving** to **walking**.

This is a much easier construction than:

I **prefer to drive**, rather than **to walk**.

Infinitive in Conditional form, but for particular preference on a certain occasion we usually use **would rather** (auxiliary, infinitive without **to**, see 2 above).

I**'d rather drive** than **walk** this afternoon.

remember   I **remember smoking** my first cigarette. (have the memory of)
I **remembered to post** the letter. (didn't forget)

Remember with gerund after the event.
Remember with infinitive before the event.

stop   He **stopped talking**. (He was silent.)
He **stopped to talk** to his friend.

This is really a use of **to** for purpose because the meaning is 'He stopped (walking because he wanted) to talk to his friend'.

try   I **tried to understand** it. (made an effort, attempted)
I **tried smoking** a cigarette for the first time. (experimented with it to see if I would like it)

● Active and Passive

1 Formation

The Passive is formed by the verb **be** in the appropriate tense and the past participle of the main verb (**used, made, built,** etc.)

	ACTIVE	PASSIVE
Present Simple	They **grow** wheat here.	Wheat **is grown** here.
Future Simple	They**'ll open** it next week.	It **will be opened** next week.
Past Simple	They **began** the castle in 1108.	The castle **was begun** in 1108.
Present Perfect	They **have restored** the tower.	The tower **has been restored.**
Modals	They **may finish** it soon.	It **may be finished** soon.
	They **must do** it again.	It **must be done** again.
Continuous forms	They**'re laying** the foundations.	The foundations **are being laid.**

The Passive sometimes occurs with an agent (**by...**) when our main interest is in a thing — a building, a book, a picture, etc:

The Mona Lisa **was painted by** Leonardo da Vinci.

but in general it is wiser to avoid it and use the Active form.

The Passive is necessary, however, in sentences where the agent is not mentioned:

The Mona Lisa **was painted** at the end of the fifteenth century.

Double object verbs: Passive forms

Some verbs can have two objects and most of them have alternative constructions.

John **gave me** some money.
John **gave** some money **to me**.

We prefer the Passive when we are not interested in the person who did the action.

Someone gave John some money. (Active)
John was given **some money.**

(We are interested in John and perhaps in the effect of the gift on him.)

Someone gave some money to John. (Active)
Some money was given to John.

(We are interested primarily in the money.)

● **Double object verbs**

Most of these verbs are found in two constructions:

He lent me some money.
He lent some money **to me.**

In the Passive two possibilities also exist:

I was lent some money.
Some money was lent to me.

In each case the first form is more common.

a) The commonest verbs of this type are:
give, guarantee, leave (money), **lend, make** (an offer, a present), **offer, owe, promise** (a reward), **read** (a story), **refuse** (a loan),

sell, send, show, teach (a language, etc.), **tell** (a story), **write** (a letter).

b) **Buy** is used in the same way but the preposition used is **for**, not **to**.

He **bought** a present **for his wife**. (He bought her a present.)

c) **Ask** is only found in the first construction with a few phrases:

I **asked him** a question (his name/the way).

Ask for is also only found in the first construction:

I **asked them for** help.
They were asked for help. (Passive)

d) **Pay** is like type a) if it refers to money, but like **ask for** if it refers to goods or services.

I **paid him** the money.
I **paid him for** the goods.
The goods were paid for. (Passive)

e) **Rent** belongs to type a), except that only the second form exists in the Passive. When the person who pays the money becomes the subject, an Active form is used.

He **rented me** the car.
He **rented** the car **to me**.
BUT I **rented** the car **from him**.
The car was rented to me/from him. (Passive)

In British English we prefer **let** for houses and only the second construction is possible.

He **let** the house **to me**.
The house was let to me. (Passive)

f) Note that **borrow** cannot be used with these constructions.

I **borrowed** the money **from him**.

g) Certain verbs are only found in the second construction. The most common are:
announce, describe, entrust, explain, introduce, propose, suggest.

He **explained** it **to me**.
It was explained to me. (Passive)

but NOT 'He explained me the subject'.

● Direct and reported speech

He said, 'I don't like onions'. (Direct)
He said **he didn't like onions.** (Reported)
She said, 'I visited my aunt yesterday'.
(Direct)
She said **that she had visited her aunt the day before**. (Reported)

Notice that when we change direct speech to reported speech, expressions of time and place (e.g. **yesterday**) often change. The tense will change also if the verb introducing the reported speech is in the past tense (e.g. **said**). Use these lists of rules for reference.

1 Tense changes

DIRECT	REPORTED
'I'm working very hard.'	He said he was working...
'I earn £100 a week.'	He said he earned...
'I'm going to change my job.'	He said he was going to...
'I'll finish it soon.'	He said he would finish it...
'I've never seen her before.'	He said he had never seen her...
'I didn't break it.'	He said he hadn't broken it.
'I can run faster than Mary.'	He said he could run faster...
'It may be too late.'	He said it might be...

2 Time and place changes

DIRECT	REPORTED
here	there
this	that
now	then
yesterday	the day before
tomorrow	the day after
last week	the week before
next week	the week after
ago	before

● Relative clauses

1 Defining relative clauses

	SUBJECT PRONOUN	OBJECT PRONOUN
Person	**who (that)**	____ **(whom) (that)**
Thing	**that (which)**	____ **(that) (which)**
Possessive	**whose**	**whose**
Prepositional		____ + **prep.** (or: prep. + **whom/which**)

a) Defining relative clauses identify the person or thing we are talking about. Without them, the sentence would be meaningless.

   The man who repaired the TV was called Fred.

b) **That** is preferred to **who** or **which** following **all, every, everything, some, something, any, anything, no, nothing, none, little, few, much, only** and superlative forms.

   The only thing that matters to him is winning.
   She is **the best secretary that** ever worked here.

c) When these clauses refer to the object of the sentence, the relative pronoun is usually omitted (contact clause).

   The man she married had a red beard.

d) It is normal to avoid pronouns in prepositional clauses either by putting the preposition at the end in a contact clause:

2 Non-defining relative clauses

That's **the man I was talking to**.

or by using **where** or **when** as relative adverbs in references to place and time:

That's **the house where I was born**. (NOT 'in which').
Do you know **the time when your plane takes off**? (NOT 'at which')

	SUBJECT PRONOUN	OBJECT PRONOUN
Person	**who**	**whom**
Thing	**which**	**which**
Possessive	**whose**	**whose**
Prepositional		prep. + **whom/which**

a) These clauses do not identify the people or things we are talking about, but give us additional information about them.

Jack Briggs, **who used to live next door to me,** has just got married.

In spoken English this information would usually be conveyed in two sentences.

You remember Jack Briggs — **he used to live next door to me**. Well, he's just got married.

b) Clauses like this are usually placed between commas but if the person or thing referred to is the object of the main clause, the relative clause can appear at the end.

I've just met Jack Briggs, **who got married last month**.

c) **Where** can be used in these clauses as a relative adverb.

Farley, **where I was born**, is a small town north of London.

d) The use of a proper name always indicates that the clause following is non-defining, not defining, because the name itself is a definition (see b) and c) above), except in cases where one of those talking may know two people or places, etc. of the same name.

Is that **the Jack Briggs who used to live next door to you**? He said that London only has 100,000 inhabitants.
— Yes, but **the London he's talking about** is in Canada.

3 Co-ordinating relative clauses

These refer to the whole of the main clause, and the only pronoun ever used is **which**.

I've just spent the weekend with Uncle Harold, **which ought to qualify me for some kind of a medal.**

Clearly, **which** does not refer to Uncle Harold but to the experience of spending the weekend with him.

Compare the following:

Someone stole her car, **which was parked outside her house**. (Non-defining, where **which** refers to the car.)
Someone stole her car, **which naturally annoyed her**. (Co-ordinating, **which** refers to the fact that the car was stolen.)

● Reflexive verbs

A number of common verbs in English are often found in reflexive constructions.

Don't do that! You'll **hurt yourself**.

These are listed below in Section 1 with notes on usage. In many cases, however, verbs whose equivalents in other languages are reflexive are more often used in English in a form employing **get** or **be** (Section 2), or are used without a reflexive form (Section 3).

1 Verbs commonly found in reflexive forms.

a) Action, pain, danger:
burn, cut, defend, hurt, kill (drown, shoot).
(But we say 'commit suicide'.)

b) Behaviour, emotion:
amuse, behave, blame, control, deceive, enjoy, express, be ashamed of, be sorry for.
(**Behave** is the only intransitive verb in these lists.)

c) Thought, speech:
consider, count, say to, talk to, tell, think.
Count and **think** are included here with the meaning of 'consider':

Consider/count/think yourself lucky.

d) Action not normally reflexive:
congratulate, educate, introduce, invite, teach.

e) Others:
can't help, prevent ,stop, weigh.

f) Idiomatic uses:
help, let, please.

Help yourself = serve yourself (with food, a drink, etc.)
Let yourself go = relax, lose inhibitions.
Please yourself =ı do as you like (usually suggesting 'if you don't agree with my suggestion').

2 Forms employing **get**, etc. instead of a reflexive form.
get accustomed to, get confused, get dressed, get engaged, get excited, get lost, get married, get tired, get upset, get wet, be self-employed, fall asleep.

3 Forms where a reflexive is not necessary or is usually incorrect.
apologise (for), decide, find out, forget, get up, hide, hurry, improve, join, move, prepare (for), remember, resign (from a job), retire (from work), shave, sit down, stand up, wake up, wash, wonder, worry.
Note, too, that we do not use a reflexive in sentences like:
I cut my hand.
I hurt my arm.
Compare this with:
I cut myself.
I hurt myself.

Stylistic reference

● Connectors and modifiers

Expressing a point of view in modern English depends primarily on the correct use of a number of expressions to connect or modify statements. You can only learn to use them properly by studying them in context and then trying to use them yourself in speech and writing. Where they occur in this section, they are printed in **bold** type.

1 Indicating or agreeing with facts

In fact, actually (= in fact), **as a matter of fact** (= in fact, though it may surprise you), **the fact (of the matter) is that ..., the truth (of the matter) is that ..., really** (= in fact).
In effect, in practice (contrasted with **in theory**).
Indeed (= in fact, but is usually used to introduce a further point).
Of course (suggesting 'as you know'), **naturally** (= of course).

2 Explaining causes and results

Because of this/that, in this/that way, for this reason, therefore.
Therefore, as a result, consequently.

3 Building up an argument

In the first place, first of all, to begin/start with, for one thing, at first sight (suggests 'superficially' and is usually contradicted by a later statement).
Secondly, in the second place, apart from (that), in addition, what's more, on top of that, besides (= and another thing), **in the same way.**
In turn (suggesting a second point deriving from the first).
Worse still (a second point worse than one already given).
On the one hand, ... on the other hand

(balanced argument). Note that **on the contrary** contradicts the previous statement.
Finally, lastly, in conclusion.

4 Expressing a personal opinion or point of view

In my opinion, in my view, from my point of view, personally, as I see it, as far as I am concerned (suggesting that others may disagree or be in a different situation), **if you ask me.**

5 Giving examples

For example, for instance.

6 Pausing for thought, or trying to say something differently to make it clearer

Well, you know, you see, let me see. I mean, I mean to say, that is (to say), in other words, or rather ...

7 Modifying what has been said

However, nevertheless, still, all the same, though (at the end of the phrase, after a comma), **even so.**

8 Modifying what you are saying

To some (a certain) extent, up to a point, more or less, at least, under the circumstances, partly, mostly, as far as I know, for all we know (but we don't know much for certain).
(All these limit the force of what is said.)
Especially, in particular, in this case, above all, let alone (= without needing to mention), **not to mention, needless to say, obviously.**
(These increase the importance of what is said, either by concentrating our attention on it or suggesting it is additional to something that is obvious.)
On the whole, in general.
(These suggest a general point of view.)
Basically, fundamentally, essentially, in essence.
(These emphasise the basic, or most important point.)

9 Doubt and certainty

Certainly, undoubtedly (indicating supposition).
Surely ...?, no doubt, (indicating supposition).

10 Honesty

Honestly, frankly, to be honest, to tell the truth.

11 Reaching conclusions

Anyway (= whatever the reasons, situation), **in any case** (= anyway), **after all** (= having taken everything into account), **as it is** (=since things are as they are).

12 Miscellaneous

And so on (= etc.).
By the way (= Now that I think of it).
We also say **That reminds me** and **While we are on the subject** in similar circumstances.

● **Do and make**

As a very general rule, we can say that **do** tends to relate to actions, **make** to causing, creating or constructing. However, here is a list of the commonest expressions, excluding phrasal verbs, for reference:

do:
better, one's best, business, damage, one's duty, evil, an exercise, a favour, good, harm, homework, an injury, a job, justice to, a kindness, an operation, repairs, right, a service, wonders, work, worse, one's worst, wrong

make:
an appointment, arrangements, attacks (on), the best (of), certain (of, about), a change, a choice, a complaint, a confession, a decision, a demand, a difference (to), a discovery, an effort, enquiries, an escape, an excuse (for), faces (at), a fool (of), a fortune, friends (with), fun (of), a fuss (about), a guess, haste, a journey, a mistake, money,

the most (of), a movement, an offer, peace, preparations, a profit, progress, a report (on, to), a request, room (for), a search (for), a speech, a success (of), sure (of), a trip, trouble (for), use (of), a voyage, war (on), way (for), (someone) welcome, work (for others).

● **Letters**

Notice the punctuation and layout of the address in the letter on page 4. In Britain people usually put their own address in the top right-hand corner, and the address of the person they are writing to, if it is a business letter, on the left-hand side. The business address is normally positioned one line below the end of the home address. Most British addresses have a postal code which is meaningless except to the Post Office — e.g. Thomas Nelson & Sons Limited, Nelson House, Mayfield Road, Walton-on-Thames, Surrey **KT12 5PL**. If you are asked to write a letter from your home address, do not translate or change the order — see the example of a letter written from Paris on page 4.

The date may be written **April 1, April 1st, 1 April** or **1st April**. Note the abbreviations **1st** (first), **2nd** (second) and **3rd** (third). All other dates are **4th, 5th,** etc. except **21st, 22nd, 23rd, 31st,** etc.

The correct way to begin any English letter is to write **Dear** followed by what you would call the person addressed if you spoke to him — **Father, Uncle Jack, Charles, Mr Smith**, etc. Not 'friend' because we usually call our friends by their names. For examination purposes it is better to avoid **My dear, Dearest** and other variations, although it is quite safe to imitate English-speaking people writing to you in real life. If you do not know a person's name, you should write **Dear Sir** or **Dear Madam**; if you write to the editor of a newspaper, **Sir**; if you write to a company, **Dear Sirs**.

Most English people end their letters to friends and relations as informally as possible — **(Yours) sincerely, affectionately**, etc. In more formal letters, **Yours sincerely** is correct when writing to a named individual. **Yours faithfully** or **Yours truly** are preferred when the letter begins **Dear Sir(s)** or **Sir**.

In the United States, the conventions are different in a number of cases. The date is written with the month before the day (**10.17.83** for **October 17th, 1983**) where the short form in Great Britain would be **17.10.83**. The punctuation after **Dear Mr Smith** is normally a colon (**:**) not a comma (**,**). If you write to a company, you normally address them as **Gentlemen**, not **Dear Sirs**. **Yours faithfully** is not used at the end of such letters. Common endings are **Yours truly, Yours sincerely, Sincerely yours.**

Answers

● Are you good at making excuses? (page 24)

Naturally this is not meant to be taken seriously, but you score 2 for a convincing excuse or lie. You score 1 for the truth. Honesty deserves some reward. You score 0 for an excuse or lie that gets you into even more trouble.

1 a) 0 And you took such a long time to tell him/her!
  b) 2
  c) 1 But get ready for the row that's going to start.
2 a) 1 We hope you enjoy your dinner!
  b) 2 They can't check it, and you may get away with it.
  c) 0 They'll invite you another day, or else keep asking Mary how her painting's getting on.
3 a) 1
  b) 0 Too quick. He'll think you're laughing at him.
  c) 2 If you can keep your face straight when you say it!
4 a) 2
  b) 1
  c) 0 Your mother, perhaps. But if it's Aunt Lucy, she ought to be dying at least.
5 a) 0 You don't really want to hear it all again, do you?
  b) 1 But don't expect to be asked again!
  c) 2 You may have to go through it again, but it's your best chance of avoiding it.

● Activity 2 (page 69)

1 C — *Oedipus Rex* by Sophocles
2 E — *Don Quixote* by Cervantes
3 D — *Huckleberry Finn* by Mark Twain.
4 B — *Othello* by Shakespeare
5 F — *Faust* by Goethe (also *Dr Faustus* by Christopher Marlowe)
6 A — *The Doll's House* by Ibsen

● Are you a Good Survivor — Psychologically? (page 92)

Check how many points you score for each of your answers from the following score guide.

	a)	b)	c)
1	0	1	2
2	0	1	2
3	1	2	0
4	1	2	0
5	2	1	0
6	1	2	0
7	2	0	1
8	1	0	2
9	0	1	2
10	1	2	0

If you scored over 16, you are capable of surviving anywhere, and with over 13, you will have few problems. From 10-13, watch your weaknesses, and from 7-10, be careful. If you scored less than 7, what are you doing out in the world on your own?

●Activity 1 (page 93)

Typical answers for each sign are as follows:

Question	1	2	3	4	5	6	7	8	9	10
Aries	c	a	a	a	c	a	a	c	b	b
Taurus	b	b	c	b	b	c	b	b	c	c
Gemini	b	a	a	b	b	b	b	c	b	c
Cancer	a	a	b	c	a	c	c	b	a	a
Leo	c	a	c	a	a	a	a	a	b	b
Virgo	b	b	b	b	b	b	c	b	c	b
Libra	b	a	c	b	b	b	c	b	c	a
Scorpio	b	b	c	a	b	c	b	a	b	a
Sagittarius	c	a	c	a	b	a	a	c	b	b
Capricorn	b	a	b	b	b	c	c	b	c	b
Aquarius	b	a	a	c	b	b	c	c	c	b
Pisces	a	c	a	c	a	c	c	b	a	a

● First Aid Quiz (page 95)

1 A If you didn't turn off the current, you would risk getting the shock yourself.
2 B If you made the patient move about too soon, you would probably cause the blood supply to his/her brain to be cut again and risk a repeat of the fainting.

3 A If you hurried the patient from a bending position into an upright, standing one, he/she might faint again.

4 B Rubbing in cream would not help to cool the burnt skin down.

5 B If you applied a tight bandage above the cut for too long, the blood supply to that part of the body would be cut off.

6 A If you tried to get the object out with your fingers (as people in a panic often do), you might only push it in further.

7 B Giving the patient food or liquids might cause vomiting, which might choke him/her. If the patient needs to have an operation, he/she should not have eaten anything beforehand. If you tried to warm the patient up with blankets or hot water bottles, you would cause the blood vessels in the skin to dilate and draw blood away from the body organs, which need the blood in an emergency.

8 B If you frightened the patient, you would only increase the state of shock.

● Were They Like Their Sun Sign? (pages 102–3)

1 William Shakespeare : Taurus
2 Elizabeth I : Virgo
3 John F. Kennedy : Gemini
4 Joan of Arc : Capricorn
5 Winston Churchill : Sagittarius
6 Charles de Gaulle : Scorpio
7 Charlie Chaplin : Aries
8 Napoleon Bonaparte : Leo
9 Charles Dickens : Aquarius
10 Sarah Bernhardt : Libra
11 Frédéric Chopin : Pisces
12 Henry VIII : Cancer

Index